PRAISE FOR *FAITH*

CH00765185

Navigating the challenges of raising pret

In *Faith That Sticks*, authors Leslie Nunnery and Tricia Goyer gently guide parents through this pivotal season of parenting, reminding us that it doesn't have to be a journey filled with uncertainty or fear; instead, it can be a time of joy and hope. Grounded in truth, *Faith That Sticks* equips parents with a deeper understanding of their preteens' developing minds while helping them plant vital seeds of faith to help their children build solid foundations for life. With practical wisdom and heartfelt encouragement, *Faith That Sticks* is a must-read for any parent seeking to create a lasting legacy of faith and love through the preteen years and beyond.

Whitney Newby
Founder & CEO of Brighter Day Press

Faith That Sticks is an essential and inspiring guide for parents navigating the complex and transformative preteen years. Addressing key challenges like mood swings, the digital age, and trials, Leslie and Tricia offer actionable steps to nurture lasting spiritual growth through prayer, Bible study, meaningful conversations, service, and strong family relationships. A must-read for every parent!

Ginger Hubbard
Bestselling author of *Don't Make Me Count to Three* and *I Can't Believe You Just Said That*; cohost of the *Parenting with Ginger Hubbard* podcast

During our frequent discussions on Leslie Nunnery's podcast, two wonderful qualities always flow naturally from Leslie. She is a caring listener who understands that connection changes human behavior more than rules. So it is no surprise that *Faith That Sticks* is infused with such grace in helping preteens internalize their faith. This is a practical, how-to guide that is a must-read.

Kirk Martin
Host, *Calm Parenting Podcast*

Faith That Sticks is practical and encouraging for every parent as they disciple their children!

Kimberly Sorgius Jones
Not Consumed Ministries

FAITH

5 Real-Life Ways to

THAT

Disciple Your Preteen

STICKS

TRICIA GOYER AND LESLIE NUNNERY

MOODY PUBLISHERS

CHICAGO

© 2025 by
TRICIA GOYER AND LESLIE NUNNERY

All rights reserved. No part of this book may be reproduced in any form without permission in writing from the publisher, except in the case of brief quotations embodied in critical articles or reviews.

Scriptures taken from the Holy Bible, New International Version®, NIV®. Copyright ©1973, 1978, 1984, 2011 by Biblica, Inc.™ Used by permission of Zondervan. All rights reserved worldwide. www.zondervan.com The "NIV" and "New International Version" are trademarks registered in the United States Patent and Trademark Office by Biblica, Inc.™

Published in association with the Books & Such Literary Management, www.booksandsuch.com.

Edited by Pamela Joy Pugh
Interior design: Puckett Smartt
Cover design: Studio Gearbox
Cover graphic of tape copyright © 2024 by Nadia Gallegos/Shutterstock (2342399753). All rights reserved.
Photo credit, Goyer: Barbie Jones

ISBN: 978-0-8024-3408-1

Originally delivered by fleets of horse-drawn wagons, the affordable paperbacks from D. L. Moody's publishing house resourced the church and served everyday people. Now, after more than 125 years of publishing and ministry, Moody Publishers' mission remains the same—even if our delivery systems have changed a bit. For more information on other books (and resources) created from a biblical perspective, go to www.moodypublishers .com or write to:

Moody Publishers
820 N. LaSalle Boulevard
Chicago, IL 60610

1 3 5 7 9 10 8 6 4 2

Printed in the United States of America

To John:

For every eye roll, deep sigh, and "I can't even" moment that parenting our preteens has thrown our way, thank you for not just enduring but embracing this wild ride with me. Your wisdom turns chaos into lessons and your partnership makes the impossible possible. I couldn't imagine anyone better to whisper "Are we there yet?" in the roller coaster of raising kids. Here's to more laughs, more love, and yes, even more teenage drama. You make it all worthwhile. With all my love and a few stolen moments of sanity. Also, for my children and grandchildren. I'm so thankful for family, for you, for faith, for togetherness.

— Tricia

To David, Camden, Payton, Lizzie Gray, and Lila:

Through the years, God has graciously shown me many ways I was not a perfect wife or mama, and I am so thankful for the grace you all have shown me as I've grown in my roles as well. You're the people I'd rather hang out with than anyone else in the world. David, thank you for walking alongside me for every new favorite stage of parenting—you're the best partner in the world! Kiddos, thank you for always giving us your hearts and staying close to us despite our mistakes and the many times you didn't understand why we were doing something. May God bless your obedience. I can't wait to see what God has in store for your own families in the days ahead.

— Leslie

CONTENTS

Part One

UNDERSTANDING PRETEENS AND WHAT THEY NEED

BEYOND MOOD SWINGS:
Preteen Identity in Crisis

ENGAGED PARENTING IN A DIGITAL AND SEXUAL WORLD:
Your Vital Role

TOGETHER THROUGH TRIALS:
Managing Anger and Stress as a Family

WELCOME TO
THE EYE-ROLL ERA

We're thrilled you've joined us—yes, right here in the thick of the pre-teen trenches where eye rolls might as well be the official communication currency. If you've ever wondered whether your child's eyes can actually get stuck mid-roll (we've all been there), you're in the right place!

We're Tricia and Leslie, and we get it—parenting preteens can feel like navigating a maze with no clear path. Every day presents new challenges, and life often feels complicated. But here's the good news: God's Word isn't. The wisdom we share in this book is built on the solid foundation of faith, rooted in God's unchanging truth. Thankfully, our loving Father didn't make it complicated. We're here to walk alongside you, with His guidance lighting the way. We want to share a little about what we've learned so you don't miss the incredible opportunity of this season with your preteens.

Not too long ago, I (Leslie) sat beside my son as he cried in frustration. My heart broke as I watched my already-bigger-than-me son struggling with new emotions, feeling out of control.

"I don't know why I keep doing such bad things," he said through the sobs. I cried out to the Lord for wisdom, knowing I was grossly insufficient for this new season.

Honestly, the infraction that caused the breakdown was rather silly. He had been caught red-handed with something that wasn't his. When he lied about it, his conscience was pricked. My big boy melted into a pool of tears.

I sat with him that day, assuring him that he wasn't broken, reminding him of God's love and my love for him. My son was experiencing growing pains on the way to becoming the man God created him to be. Eventually, we broke our huddle and returned to the day's regular activities.

When his tears first came, I was scared, not understanding what I was dealing with. I felt so sorry for my son that I thought my heart would break. With the benefit of hindsight, I am filled with gratitude. I'm thankful I was the one who was privileged to hold him, comfort him, and assure him. I'm grateful for patience and wisdom from God.

God used that moment and countless others to forge a tight relationship between me and my boy. Although it happened a decade ago, my heart pricks as if it were yesterday. Since that day, God has led me to speak into the lives of other moms through the Teach Them Diligently conferences that my husband and I host—and through podcasts, books, and our TTD 365 Community group. I love offering insight and encouragement. This insight doesn't come from pride, thinking I've got all the answers. Instead, I'm a mom who's been scared that I'll mess up. Moreover, I haven't always gotten it right.

The challenges of parenting preteens include dealing with their fluctuating emotions, navigating disciplinary situations, and managing their desire for independence while maintaining family traditions and expectations. Preteens may also experience peer pressure and be influenced by social media. However, there are opportunities to build strong relationships by engaging your children at a heart level, asking questions about their thoughts and emotions, and planting seeds of faith and values. Honest communication and a positive family culture can also help develop their identity. Yet, unique children from various family backgrounds struggle with identity in different ways.

I (Tricia) first saw the grinning faces of four of my daughters through an email from an adoption caseworker. After raising three children to adulthood, John and I felt called to expand our family. In my husband's words, "God doesn't call us to a life of comfort." This led us to adopt seven children, including a teen and her three preteen sisters.

Parenting these ages is hard enough, yet we were soon parenting preteens who'd faced trauma and rejection. It was tough! Yet, the good news is, to pass on faith, we didn't have to do anything different than what we'd already been doing with our kids: spending time with them, sharing God's love in simple ways, and teaching our children to invite Him into every part of their lives.

Leslie and I want to share a little about what we've learned within these pages so that you don't miss the incredible opportunity of passing on faith during these years.

The key points we'll be sharing include:

> Understanding the stages of development your preteen is experiencing.

> Realizing we live in a digital age and learning how to navigate it with preteens.

> Creating a safe and supportive family culture.

> Modeling faith and involving children in spiritual practices such as prayer and Bible reading.

> Building a foundation of faith strong enough to stick with children throughout their lives.

I (Tricia) am barely out of parenting the preteen years. Our biological children are now in their thirties. Yet our adopted children are between the ages of fourteen and twenty-four. I've been homeschooling for thirty years, which is a long time, yet I am so thankful for all the time we've had to pass on faith.

My (Leslie's) children are now 25, 23, 21, and 18, and I've discovered that even when I'm not perfect, I can seek God and draw closer to my kids instead of running away in fear.

My husband, David, and I have always believed that discipleship is the core of family life, and we've done our best to live that out. Still, the preteen years were some of the hardest. We've heard the same from thousands of moms at our conferences. Yet, when we really commit to showing our kids love, and we set clear priorities to pass on truth and hope in God, we help our children develop a faith that sticks—not just for a season but for a lifetime.

It's a blessing to have a front-row seat to watch our children develop from precocious children to young people and then to become the adults God has created them to be. Stand in awe of this opportunity! We can do this together. Let's get started.

Chapter One

BEYOND MOOD SWINGS

Preteen Identity in Crisis

magine standing in a room full of mirrors, each reflecting a different version of yourself—this is what preteens experience as they start to question their identity: *Who am I? What makes me unique? Am I defined by my talents, looks, or popularity?* These questions are a normal part of their development. They look to their gifts, talents, appearance, and social standing for answers. The allure of name-brand clothes, the desire to emulate a favorite singer or social media influencer, and the need to be liked by peers all play into their search for significance and value.

One thing I (Leslie) learned from my youngest daughter, Lila, is the importance of grounding one's identity in an enduring foundation and not just in achievements. An excellent volleyball player by seventh grade, the game had become an idol for her. Then, during a mid-season warmup, a freak accident and a broken finger ended her season. She was devastated, mostly because this changed her identity.

Lila has spoken about how God used that injury to help her realize that if volleyball were to go away forever, she would still have value as a child of God. *He* had a plan for her. That's a pretty valuable life lesson to learn when you're young!

A PRETEEN'S REALITY

Leslie

What do you remember about your preteen years? I hadn't thought about mine for years until I started working on this project. My family moved three times before my teen years. I went to three schools in three different states, constantly making new friends and having to adjust. I often felt lost and out of place.

I also felt uncomfortable with how I looked. I have very curly hair and, at my request, my mom allowed me to cut my hair short and layered. I looked like a poodle. Add both of those things with the insecurity and all the emotions that come with being a preteen, and I struggled.

Once a guy I liked came and sat beside me at a revival meeting we were both attending. I was pleased that he wanted to be by me. His presence made my heart skip a beat . . . until he pulled out his wallet and asked me if I wanted to see a picture of his girlfriend.

Start with Empathy

As I was reminiscing about being a preteen, it dawned on me that as I was raising my kids, I didn't consider my struggles at that age. I wish I had. It would have made it a lot easier to understand my kids' challenges better. Empathy bridges the gap between our past and our children's present. When we remember how awkward or confused *we* felt, we are more likely to have compassion with our kids.

Take a minute and think back to your reality as a preteen. That will give you more empathy and insight as you look at ways to love your kiddos well through this time. Empathy will guide you as you disciple your children and shepherd their hearts.

The Bible tells us in 1 Peter 3 that husbands must dwell (or be fully present) with their wives with knowledge and understanding. Husbands should take the time to learn what blesses or distresses their wives and keep those things in mind as they dwell together. As parents, we must do the same regarding our children. We can take the time to understand them better so we can parent them well. Being fully present means learning to see the world through their eyes. Of course it's easier said than done, especially with all the high emotions that come with the preteen years.

It's the Brain!

We've heard about the hormonal rushes and changes taking place inside our children during their preteen years and the havoc that wreaks on them—and us! But it's not just the hormones that are rapidly changing. Many of the changes that happen during these years are linked to the brain. Researchers are learning that although hormone levels are high at the beginning of puberty, it's the brain changes that play an even greater role in mood swings.

During the preteen years and throughout adolescence, the brain undergoes significant reorganization and maturation, especially in areas related to social relationships, emotion processing, risk-taking, and experiencing rewards. The limbic system, which processes emotions, causes adolescents to be more emotional and reactive, leading to more pronounced ups and downs. Meanwhile, the prefrontal cortex, responsible for reasoning, decision-making, and impulse control, continues to mature into the twenties. As the connections between the prefrontal cortex and the limbic system improve, adolescents become

> **Just as our children are sprouting up physically, they're also sprouting up mentally. They're just as awkward in growing into their new way of thinking.**

better at controlling emotions and making rational decisions.[1] What does this mean? There are a lot of years when our children's brains are changing. We often wonder why they're doing what they're doing, and they might not even know!

While a person's brain is not fully developed until their twenties, some of the biggest changes are happening during the preteen years. Around age eleven, a child's brain function is in hyperdrive as they are developing more complex thinking abilities.

Consider someone who's had a growth spurt. They are clumsy and awkward because they haven't quite grown into their limbs or adapted to their new height. We can see those challenges and accept them for what they are. But just as our children are sprouting up physically, they're also sprouting up mentally. They're just as awkward in growing into their new way of thinking. Too often, though, instead of reacting to *them* in an understanding way, we react to the awkwardness, anger, or frustration, which reinforces the insecurity they already feel. It is imperative that, as parents, we understand what is going on physiologically with them, so we can be careful to react appropriately and not make faulty assumptions as we parent them.

Understanding our children begins with remembering our own journey. And being fully present means learning to see the world through their eyes. It's remembering that they're still trying to discover their identity. It's knowing that most preteens feel awkward and out of place.

How would the way you engage with your preteen change if you were assuming that their behavior and emotional outbursts were related to brain changes rather than rebellion or hormones?

The brain changes during this time are profound, leading to out-sized emotions and intense feelings. Puberty can make preteens more emotionally sensitive than ever before. As a mom, I was prepared for this with my girls, but my boys' emotional swings during puberty caught me off guard! (I had never been a preteen boy, after all.)

Preteens experience new emotions and often don't know how to handle them. Rash behavior, angry outbursts, unexpected crying, and heightened sensitivity to others' emotions are not uncommon. Your response as a parent matters. Don't let fear, frustration, or anger lead your reactions, as your child will feel these more acutely during this time.

Preteens often express anger when they are frustrated or angry with themselves. It's easy to think they're becoming angry people, which feeds our parenting fear of losing them. Instead, give them time to settle down. This may be a few minutes or a few hours. Engaging with them calmly afterward can lead to more constructive conversations than pushing hard in the heat of the moment.

On the flip side, you may find your preteen becoming more funny, creative, curious, and sweet. You get glimpses of the young adult they're becoming, even as you see traces of the child they were. It's a delightful time!

They're also very sensitive about their mistakes. Many parents have shared how their preteens struggle with guilt. But this is an opportunity to teach them about grace and forgiveness. If they haven't accepted Christ's salvation, introduce them to His grace. If they're already believers, help them understand the depth of His forgiveness. Parenting through the preteen years can be emotionally intense, but as a parent who is intentional in reaching your children's hearts, building strong relationships with them, and pointing them to Jesus, you can offer stability and love. What a wonderful gift that is!

Sensitive Discipline

Preteens are often self-conscious and overly aware of their own shortcomings. David and I found that even the way we disciplined our children had to change from our approach when they were younger. It's important not to embarrass them, especially in front of their peers or siblings. We can do this by talking down to them or speaking to them harshly in front of others. Preteens are very sensitive to these actions. This can put a wedge between you and your child, leading to bitterness. Rather than leading to reconciliation, this approach could harden their hearts, damaging their self-esteem and your relationship with them. Our mission as parents is to reach the heart of our child and instill a lasting faith. This means constantly adapting our methods and tools.

You're Not Living with a Stranger

Ever feel like your preteen is a stranger in your house? In addition to growth in brain development, children at this age are on a quest for identity. They're eager to figure out who they are, what they like, and how they fit into the world. This often results in them "trying on" different personalities and looks. As their brain develops, they're exploring who they are outside of just being part of your family, which can mean new hobbies, music, and even the way they talk. It's all part of growing up.

To us parents, this "trying on personas" can seem fake, frustrating, and even scary. We fear they'll experiment their way into trouble. But like the creative process (where you work through many bad ideas before landing on a good one), this experimentation is normal and necessary. As parents, we can lovingly guide them through these phases. We can see these "rough drafts" of their personality as opportunities to guide them.

Asking questions that help preteens process their beliefs and manage new relationships is a crucial and rewarding part of parenting during this stage.

This is a prime time to help them think biblically about their identity and build a deeper relationship as you explore their interests together. You'll also be there to comfort your preteens when their peers don't react well to some of their experiments. Asking questions that help them process their beliefs and manage new relationships is a crucial and rewarding part of parenting during this stage.

THE WORLD'S MESSAGES

Tricia

In a world where identity is shaped by a whirlwind of external influences, the preteen years are particularly vulnerable to confusion and uncertainty. The voices of media, influencers, and peers are louder than ever, often leaving our children feeling torn between authenticity and conformity. As their guides, it's our privilege—and our responsibility—to help them find clarity amidst the noise, grounding them in truth while encouraging their God-given uniqueness to shine through.

In today's world, answers to questions about identity are often dictated by powerful external voices. Media, advertisements, celebrities, influencers, and peer groups bombard our preteens with messages about what they should look like, how they should behave, and who they should be. These messages can be conflicting and overwhelming. One moment, they are told to embrace their individuality, and the next, they are shown images of an ideal they must conform to.

On top of conflicting messages about appearance and behavior, there are also complex discussions about gender, identity, and self-worth that can further confuse their developing minds. The digital age brings a constant stream of information and opinions, making it difficult for preteens to discern truth from fiction. Since these are issues that parents ask us about most, we will talk more about them in chapter 2.

As parents, our first response might be to shield our children from these influences. And while we can try, it's impossible to shield our preteens from all the messages completely—they're everywhere. A more effective approach is to walk alongside them with empathy and understanding. Recognize that your preteen is not just acting out or being difficult—they are genuinely trying to make sense of the overwhelming noise coming at them from every direction. Their brain is still developing and is capable of incredible growth and adaptation, but it is also particularly vulnerable.

Imagine being bombarded with constant messages about your worth and identity while trying to figure out the basics of who you are. It's like trying to build a house in the middle of a hurricane. Your preteen needs your empathy, not your frustration.

Grounding Them in Truth

Preteens often face additional emotional challenges from outside influences, such as friends experiencing parental divorce, or bullying on social media. These issues can be overwhelming for them, as they aren't equipped to handle such heavy emotions at their age. This is why the relationship with your child is so important. Investing time, listening, and having meaningful conversations are critical.

The realities our preteens face today are vastly different from what we experienced at their age. Even within a single family, younger siblings might experience more intense peer pressure and all-hours access to others via cellphones. Protecting them from too much access to influences apart from the home is one of the best gifts we can give. Setting boundaries around family time can protect them from the stress of constant peer interaction. For example, you might choose not to allow cellphones at this age. We can't create a bubble around them, so it's important to prepare them for these encounters. Discussing potential situations ahead of time and providing guidance can help them navigate these interactions more effectively.

This is where our role as parents becomes crucial. We need to be the stable, loving presence that helps ground them in truth. Remind them that their value does not come from their talents, looks, or popularity. Their worth is inherent because they are created in the image of God.

Encourage them to explore their interests and talents but help them understand that these are not the ultimate source of their identity. Their gifts and abilities are given by God for a purpose, but they do not define who they are. While it's natural for preteens to want to be liked and fit in, their value is not dependent on the approval of others.

Addressing the Noise

Help your preteen navigate the noise by teaching them to filter the messages they receive. Equip them to evaluate the media they consume critically. Discuss openly the pressures they feel from social media, peers, and even from within. Validate their feelings and provide a safe space for them to express their doubts and fears.

Introduce them to biblical truths about identity and worth. Help them see themselves through God's eyes—loved, valued, and purposeful. Share stories from the Bible where God used unlikely people for great purposes, not because of their outward appearance or societal status, but because of their hearts and willingness to follow Him.

Use this time to build a deeper relationship with your preteen. Engage in activities they enjoy and show genuine interest in their world. Ask open-ended questions that encourage them to think about their beliefs and values. Be the one who comforts them when they feel rejected or misunderstood by their peers.

Remember, your preteen is looking for a safe place to land in the midst of their identity storm. Be that refuge for them. Offer them the stability and love they need to navigate this challenging yet exciting time in their lives.

THE INFLUENCE OF THE FAITH COMMUNITY

Tricia

As we explore the preteen years and the quest for identity, it's essential to understand the pivotal role certain events play in shaping who we become with our talents and in our faith. Concerning my talents, one major marker for me was our move to a new house, which was just a mile away from the library, while I was in elementary school. As a struggling reader placed in special reading classes, the proximity to the library opened up a whole new world for me. I began reading voraciously, devouring books, and eventually developed a deep love for reading. This passion later inspired my dream of becoming an author. Looking back, I realize this was part of discovering who God created me to be.

There was also an awakening of my faith during these years, and it was—in a large part—due to the community of believers who wrapped around our family when I was a preteen. I vividly remember when my mom and grandma became Christians. It was when I was in second or third grade, and we started going to church for the first time. Prior to this, I hadn't grown up in a church environment, and my stepdad wasn't a Christian, so it was all new to me. This shift brought significant changes in my life.

Our church community played such a critical role during these formative years. The church body embraced us wholeheartedly. I still remember my Sunday school teacher, Margo, who was a constant presence as her students navigated those awkward preteen years. She encouraged us to memorize Scripture, rewarding us with stickers, prizes, and even special outings. Margo saw me, recognized my awkwardness, and valued me for who I was. She made a lasting impact by helping me feel seen and loved in a time when I felt most awkward and uncertain about myself.

The church community wasn't just about Sunday school and Scripture memorization. The adults in the congregation talked to me, showed interest in my life, and provided a sense of belonging and stability. These interactions were foundational, shaping my identity and faith more deeply than I realized at the time.

As preteens, we often search for a mirror that reflects something familiar, something reassuring. For me, that mirror was the church community. It became a place where I could step away from the pressures of fitting in and simply be myself. In a world where I was constantly measuring my worth by external standards—whether it was what I wore or how popular I was—my church family saw beyond that. They reminded me that my identity wasn't found in the shifting opinions of others but in something far more steadfast: my relationship with Christ.

My Sunday school teacher and so many others reflected back to me a version of myself rooted in love and grace, reminding me that my worth was already secure, regardless of what I wore or how many friends I had.

Years later, at seventeen, I found myself pregnant, engulfed in depression and isolation. Despite drifting away from the church during my teenage years, the seeds of truth planted in my heart began to stir. Those Scriptures, a legacy from my mother's dedication to church and Margo's Sunday school lessons, became a beacon of hope during my darkest times.

One particularly low day, feeling forsaken by my boyfriend and friends, I reflected on the joy I had once felt in Sunday school. Recalling John 3:16, the first Scripture I had memorized, reminded me of God's love and sacrifice. It was then that I realized prayer was not just about seeking change in circumstances but in seeking a transformation within myself.

In my despair, I dared to believe God hadn't forsaken me either. A simple, heartfelt prayer marked the turning point toward peace and light in my heart, reaffirming God's love and the promise of eternal life through belief in Him.

Even though I faced challenges during my teenage years, the foundation laid during my preteen years brought me back to my faith as a pregnant teen. Those seeds of faith took root even after years of being trampled on and neglected!

THE INFLUENCE OF FAITH AT HOME

Leslie

I can also chime in for the importance of a strong faith foundation. Amidst all the changes and upheaval in my life, my family remained a constant source of stability. As I've said, we moved frequently, constantly starting over in new places, with new schools and new churches. Despite this impermanence, my mom and dad ensured that my sister and I had a firm faith foundation. They consistently pointed us to Jesus, helping us understand why they believed what they believed.

Much like those mirrors that reflected so many different versions of myself, each new move presented a chance to see life from a new angle, to reimagine who I was in unfamiliar surroundings. Yet, in the midst of those constant changes, my parents' faithfulness provided the one unchanging reflection I needed—who I was in Christ. No matter how many schools or churches we attended, no matter how different the people or the environments, my parents' unwavering commitment to God remained my compass. They helped me see beyond the temporary—new friendships, new challenges—and focus on the eternal truths that anchored my identity. Through their example, I learned to embrace the many facets of my life while holding fast to the one mirror that never changes: my reflection in God's eyes.

And you can do the same for your preteens. Your unwavering support and guidance during these years are crucial. Even amidst the chaos, you can provide a sense of security and stability that will anchor your children. As a parent, you can help transition your preteen from a little child who simply follows, to someone who can think independently and develop his or her own beliefs and identity in Christ.

* * *

Let's embrace our evolving role with empathy and wisdom, recognizing the incredible opportunity we have to shape their future. By walking alongside them, we can help them become confident, grounded individuals who know their worth in Christ. What a privilege it is to be part of this journey, guiding our children as they discover who God created them to be.

Chapter Two

ENGAGED PARENTING IN A DIGITAL AND SEXUAL WORLD

Your Vital Role

Have you ever experienced something like this? Picture a sunny Saturday afternoon, the park buzzing with laughter and children playing. You're watching your preteens dart across the field with their friends, their faces beaming with joy. On the park bench, sipping coffee, you can't help but think about how different their world is compared to the one you grew up in. The realities facing today's preteens are vastly different from even a decade ago.

PARENTS AND FEAR

Leslie

All these changes can be alarming to us as parents. However, we cannot parent by fear. Instead, we must parent by faith. Do what God has called you to do and trust that He will take care of the ones you love. When you feel overwhelmed by social media, peer pressure, and everything else coming at your kids, turn that anxiety into an opportunity to cast your cares on the Lord, as instructed in 1 Peter 5:7: "Cast all your anxiety on him because he cares for you." Acknowledge the fear that is welling up inside you and ask God to direct your steps and give you wisdom. James 1:5 promises that He will give wisdom liberally when you ask.

The preteen years can be a time when fear rushes in for many parents. My oldest two are boys, and during this season, the fear I struggled with almost paralyzed me. I became ineffective as a parent because I constantly worried about all the dangers they would face, especially online, and all the things I couldn't protect them from. This fear overwhelmed me, and it was to the point where I even avoided necessary conversations with my children. Thankfully, God convicted me of my fear before it caused serious harm to my children.

Philippians 4:6 tells us, "Do not be anxious about anything, but in every situation, by prayer and petition, with thanksgiving, present your requests to God." This includes raising preteens. If you don't deal with issues when they are preteens, you will likely face the same issues later. When your children are out on their own, they can choose what they want. If we work on their hearts at these ages, we have the opportunity to be thankful, not fearful. Be thankful for the opportunity to address these issues while your children are still at home.

One thing I have often done is pray with open palms, saying, "Lord, these kids are Yours. This situation is Yours. This is really hard." This mindset helps us use difficult moments as opportunities to discuss God's standards with our kids, which builds a foundation for future (and sometimes even more difficult) conversations.

Satan wants to instill fear during this time because of the incredible opportunities we have to guide our children. If he can make us too afraid to get involved, he knows he has a better chance of influencing them when they are teenagers and young adults. If we fight through that fear and have those crucial conversations now, we lay a foundation of trust and counsel that will serve them well in the future.

When Fear Leads to Distrust

During this season of raising preteens, I had a sense of dread that my boys would fall into all kinds of horrible traps from the enemy, and I found myself growing increasingly distrustful of them. My mind played tricks on me and my imagination went wild, and our relationship took a short-term beating for it. My very sensitive preteens recognized that I didn't regard them as trustworthy as I used to, and they were hurt by it.

There will be times when your child loses your trust through his actions, but parents often struggle with skepticism about their child based on what they are fearful they will do or participate in. If you find yourself feeling that way, now's the time to make that right with your son or daughter. Explain to them that you were allowing fear to cause you to react foolishly. Talk to them about how even parents need to be reining in our thoughts so they're in line with what we know to be true. Times like these when you acknowledge your mistakes offer you great relationship-building times with them and strengthen trust in the long run.

WHAT THE WORLD IS TELLING YOU

Leslie

If you look at pop culture and the way that the world wants to make you think of this age group, you would assume that preteens don't want to be anywhere near their parents because they're so embarrassed by them. In almost every movie or TV show, parents are portrayed as rather stupid, dated, and awkward. Honestly, I'd be embarrassed by most of them as well.

Far too many parents take their cues from that mindset, and they allow their children to do likewise, often out of the fear that intruding in their lives too much will cost them a relationship with their child in the long run. Nothing could be further from the truth. The prince of this world is having a heyday with families by deceiving parents into pulling back or transitioning to being their child's friend instead of offering them the truth, love, safety, and emotional stability that is so critical as they develop.

God didn't design our families to dissolve or our influence to stop when our kids became preteens.

You see, God didn't design our families to dissolve or our influence to stop when our kids became preteens. Sadly, many parents back off and grieve the changes they see in their children during this phase instead of continuing to engage in their lives as they did when they were younger—playing games, having family dinners, going on outings and vacations. They stop taking advantage of the unique position they've been given to help shepherd their children through this phase of their growth.

This leaves our kids at the mercy of others who are very willing to fill that void, and culturally, we're seeing the fruit of that. Issues that have always proved difficult for preteens are magnified now that so many of them have access to so much media and information right at hand. Issues like distraction, bullying, addiction, pornography, and more are impacting our children even more than they have historically, and rates of youth anxiety, depression, and suicide are rising at alarming rates.[2]

Good relationships with parents and families give preteens better emotional support, the security and safety of healthy boundaries, and protection against a wide range of risky behaviors.

You'll recall that in chapter 1, we looked at some of the changes your child is going through during this time to help you better understand them. But stay engaged and consistent no matter how much they push boundaries or test your patience. The short-term benefits for them will be notable, and you'll find that when this relatively brief season of their lives is over, they'll come out on the other side with an even stronger relationship with you than before.

Continue doing what God has called you to do: parenting and disciplining your children with love, going for their hearts all along the way. There's no pause button on God's call for parents while your kids go through this preteen time. So stay consistent and stay engaged. They may bristle at it, but they will thank you for it later.

IT'S A DIFFERENT WORLD

Tricia

Our children's world is one where access to media and information can fit right into their pockets. The same device they use to text me from the community swimming pool also exposes them to the vast, unfiltered expanse of the internet. Distraction, bullying, addiction, and exposure to inappropriate content are issues that have always existed, but they are now amplified by the digital age.

This kind of exposure to darkness definitely creates problems, as statistics tell us a worrying story. According to the American Academy of Pediatrics, "national surveillance data suggests that roughly 7–8% of adolescents attempt suicide each year, and roughly 17% report serious suicidal ideation." In 2020, suicide was the second leading cause of death for five-to-nine-year-olds and the second leading cause of death for ten-to-fourteen-year-olds.[3] These numbers are alarming and underscore the importance of our role as parents in our children's lives. We must tread carefully, not to scare but to inform and underscore our vital role in providing support and guidance to our preteens.

Even secular research finds that relationships with parents and families provide preteens with essential emotional support, security, and safety. As we've stressed, ongoing positive family connections are protective factors against a wide range of health risk behaviors. This is the beacon of hope we need to focus on.

Relationship Rules

Over the years, John and I have used tools to help block inappropriate content. Some worked better than others. Also, since we adopted older kids, they'd already been exposed to a lot. It wasn't as if we were trying to keep our children from any exposure. Instead, we were trying to stop them from accessing things they'd already been exposed to.

Relationship trumps rules every time. Kids know when you really care and when you have their best interests in mind.

This experience made it clear that as parents we needed to be proactive regarding our children's online access. We also needed to keep on top of things to make sure they were working. Setting up safeguards isn't enough. We must be diligent to check on our kids often.

It's important to teach our kids to question the credibility of online content and not to share personal information. One evening, my son proudly showed me a new game he wanted to download. After a bit of research with my husband, we found out it was a scam. That experience taught my son a valuable lesson in online vigilance. The saying "It's better to be safe than sorry" is 100 percent true when it comes to anything online.

Teaching responsible online behavior is just as important as choosing what to look at and how to navigate good sites. John and I often talk about privacy, online etiquette, and critical thinking.

While we won't provide step-by-step ways to keep kids safe online (there are many books on that specific topic!), we do address this as an important topic. In fact, our overall goal is to help you learn effective ways to disciple your children, to spend time with them, and to have conversations so that these topics flow naturally out of our everyday lives. Creating rules and putting limits will only go so far. Our desire is that you connect with the heart of your preteen. Relationship trumps rules every time. Kids know when you really care and when you have their best interests in mind.

PRETEENS AND DIGITAL CONTENT
Leslie

Many kids I grew up with who attended a Christian school went through a rebellious period after high school when they were out of their parents' homes. My sister and I hadn't felt the need to show our independence that way. One primary reason is that our parents took the time to help us understand why we believed what we believed. Once we reached our preteens, Mom and Dad didn't rely on simply giving us rules because they said so. They taught us why those rules were in place. As a parent, I have tried to do the same thing.

Most preteens today have relatively easy access to digital content. Even if you don't allow your child to have a device of their own at this stage, most of their friends will, and they are likely to be impacted by it. Both Tricia and I homeschooled our children, but we could not entirely insulate them from digital content, and neither can you. Therefore, now is the perfect time to educate them and give them ammunition to face temptation or peer pressure. Help them understand what's appropriate and what isn't, covering both content and time spent engaging with it. Your children need you to prepare them to navigate these challenges because we cannot insulate them completely.[4]

First and foremost, setting age-appropriate boundaries is critical. We decided that our children could start using social media around the age of thirteen, but even then, it depended on their maturity level. For example, one of my daughters was very responsible and aware of the potential risks, so we felt comfortable letting her start at that age. In contrast, one of our sons needed more time to understand and handle those challenges.

Monitoring and limiting access was another essential step. We used parental control software to keep an eye on their online activities and set restrictions on their devices. It was also understood that we would always have access to their passwords to give another level of accountability. I remember one incident when my son stumbled upon a site with inappropriate content. Thanks to our monitoring, we caught it early and used it as a teachable moment.

Make Offline More Exciting Than Online

Encouraging offline activities helps maintain a healthy balance. We've always prioritized outdoor play, reading, hobbies, and family time. Our family organized a family camping trip where we left all devices at home. You can easily do that with museum visits or even walks around the neighborhood. These are wonderful opportunities for the kids to reconnect with creativity, nature, and each other away from screens.

SEXUAL IDENTITY AND PRETEENS
Tricia

As parents, we are often left grappling with the overwhelming number of issues preteens face in today's media-saturated world. And just when we think we've navigated one challenge, another rises to the surface, perhaps one of the most sensitive and complex topics of all—questions surrounding their sexual identity.

It's not hard for young people to stumble across inappropriate sexual material online. Even if they don't, other children do—and these other kids are quick to share what they see or learn. Because of this, preteens may begin to explore and question their sexual orientation and gender identity, which can be confusing and sometimes distressing. It is crucial for parents to approach these conversations with sensitivity and unconditional love. This can be hard, especially when alarm signals are going off in our heads.

I've discovered one of the best ways to address this is to listen and ask questions. When one of our preteens commented to me that she thought she was bisexual, the first thing that came out of my mouth was, "No, you're not." She seemed shocked that I seemed so confident in my answer.

"How do you know?" she asked, genuinely surprised.

"First, I've heard you talk about boys that are cute. Second, there are hormones racing through your body, which can make things confusing." Then I paused. "But why do you think that?" I asked.

"Well, I think other girls are pretty," she admitted.

"All girls think girls are pretty. We notice each other—how someone dresses or looks. That doesn't change anything about our sexual orientation. I notice when my friends look especially cute all the time, but I still love and am dedicated to your dad. Noticing how someone looks doesn't change that."

As I pondered this conversation, I looked into it more deeply, and John and I discovered that a friend of her older sister had been reaching out in inappropriate ways. Talking about it in simple ways allowed us to continue the conversation. I didn't get upset or overreact, and I knew my daughter appreciated that. She also appreciated when we reached out to the older girl and asked her to stop her advances toward our daughter. And I knew that the simple facts I had stated about "All girls think girls are pretty" really stuck with her, because years later I heard her repeating that to a younger sibling.

This reminded me again that preteens are searching for their identity during that time, and although they may hear a lot of things from the world or others, they will listen to us when we speak reason and truth. It was also a good reminder to me to pray for my children even more during this time.[5]

* * *

We're consistently reminded that while the world around our children is constantly changing, the fundamental need for parental guidance and love remains the same. By modeling faith, setting appropriate boundaries, and maintaining open lines of communication, we can provide our preteens with the tools they need to navigate their increasingly complex world. It's about more than just surviving these years; it's about thriving and helping our children become resilient, compassionate, and confident individuals. As parents, we have the privilege and responsibility to guide them through these formative years, ensuring they grow up with a strong foundation of faith and values that will serve them well throughout their lives.

Chapter Three

TOGETHER THROUGH TRIALS

Managing Anger and Stress as a Family

A nger is such a powerful and common emotion that we wanted to devote some time discussing it. The preteen years, with all the changes our children are going through, is a time when anger can bubble over. If you can help your child learn to break that cycle, you will be passing on tools that will stick throughout life. We'll also briefly touch on a couple of other foundational tools, such as addressing pressures preteens face and the importance of family togetherness.

BREAKING THE CYCLE OF ANGER IN PRETEENS

Tricia

The flash of anger in my tween daughter's eyes surprised me. We were camping, and my six-year-old had just burned her finger on hot ash. As I treated the wound, my preteen daughter approached. "I hurt myself, too," she said with attitude. "Last night when we were making s'mores."

"Hold on," I said. I tried not to show my frustration as my younger child was still screaming. "I need to help your sister first." This was the first I'd heard of the preteen's burn.

My preteen's anger flared. "You always help her first! You don't care about me!" She rushed back to our cabin as I finished bandaging the six-year-old's hand.

Dreading the confrontation ahead, I walked back to the cabin. I anticipated pleas and demands from me, mounting anger and accusations from her. There had to be a better way to manage these cycles of anger.

Understanding the Angry Cycle

Once a child is angry, it's easy for them to stay in a cycle of thoughts, emotions, and physical responses that feed their rage. Here's what the angry cycle looks like:

1. Trigger Event: Something causes pain or distress, setting off the anger.

2. Trigger Thoughts: The pain triggers thoughts focusing anger on someone else, like feeling misunderstood or less valued.

3. Emotional Response: These thoughts lead to feelings of frustration, rejection, or rage.

4. Physical Response: Emotions cause physical reactions like a flushed face, tense jaw, and clenched fists.

5. Behavioral Response: The combined thoughts, emotions, and physical reactions lead to a fight, flight, or freeze response.

Stopping the Angry Cycle

Lecturing or disciplining children in the midst of their anger often doesn't work. An emotional, angry preteen may be as irrational as an emotional, angry toddler. To help, we must first stop the angry cycle. Use calming phrases instead of escalating the interaction:[6]

"I see you're angry."

"I'm sorry that happened. I'll be here to talk when you're ready."

"I get angry too. How can I help?"

"When you're ready, I can tell you how I handle things when I get mad."

"It's okay to be angry but think about how you act next. Make good choices."

"I understand you're angry. Can you try to understand my point?"

When I acknowledge my children's anger and make myself available, they see that I'm paying attention. They want to make good choices but need extra guidance and appreciate my offer to help.

Training Kids to Manage Their Anger

Understanding the physical reactions to anger helps kids break the cycle. The adrenal glands flood the body with stress hormones, preparing it for physical exertion. Heart rate, blood pressure, and respiration increase.

Teach children to manage their anger using the three R's:

1. Recognize: Identify the trigger thought before the emotion. Write down and review common trigger thoughts like "She doesn't care" or "This isn't fair."

2. Reflect: Evaluate the accuracy of the thought. Encourage them to question whether their thoughts are true.

3. Redirect: Replace the faulty thought with the truth. Philippians 4:8 encourages us to think about what is true, honorable, and praiseworthy. Help your child focus on these truths.

By teaching our kids to catch, check, and change their trigger thoughts, we help them manage anger and develop healthier responses. This equips them to stop the cycle of anger and make better choices.[7]

Understanding and Addressing Preteen Anger

Anger in preteens can stem from a variety of sources, and as parents, it's essential to go beyond simply telling our children to calm down. Instead, we need to identify the underlying causes of their anger. If your child seems uncomfortable or acts angry around a particular person, don't ignore their reaction. It's crucial to dig deeper and understand why. There is always a reason behind their behavior, and if something in your gut tells you there is a problem, you're likely right.

For instance, a friend of mine noticed her preteen daughter becoming awkward and angry whenever a certain adult male friend was around. The mother observed that her daughter wasn't her usual carefree self. After discussing her daughter's reactions to this man, she discovered that he had been treating her daughter inappropriately. The young girl had been too scared to tell her parents initially, but thankfully, her mother trusted her instincts and pressed in, uncovering the truth behind her daughter's anger.

It's vital to assure your children that if they ever need to share something that has happened, you will always believe them. Fear of not being believed or uncertainty about how to express what's happening can keep many kids silent. Let your children know that you will listen, care, and take action.

I'm grateful that I've learned to see my children's anger as a form of communication—a way for them to express their needs and struggles—rather than just viewing it as a behavior problem. It reminds me that children who act out are often in distress and don't know how to manage their frustration or anger effectively. By understanding this, we can better support and guide them through their emotions.

Dealing with Anxiety

It's crucial for us to teach preteens that having emotions is not wrong. God made us to experience and express emotions. This time in their lives offers a valuable opportunity to help children understand their emotions better and learn to respond with biblical principles.

When a child is dealing with anxiety, what may seem like a minor problem can escalate into a significant outburst. One of our daughters often felt anxious about her homework. When she encountered a problem she didn't understand, her anxiety would trigger her "fight or flight" instinct—usually leading to a fight. She'd lash out, refuse to do her work, throw her pencils, and verbally attack others in the room. Initially, I thought this was simply a behavior problem that needed to be controlled. However, when I realized that anxiety was the trigger, I adopted a different approach. I assured her that I was there to help and that she didn't need to become anxious. I also taught her some calming techniques to use when she felt anxiety mounting.

Anxiety can be easy to spot in some children and harder to detect in others. Signs of anxiety include excessive worry, trouble sleeping, irritability, and difficulty concentrating. I knew one of my teen daughters was dealing with generalized anxiety when she confided in me, saying, "I always feel that something bad is going to happen." Unlike situational anxiety caused by something like homework, it turned out that this daughter's anxiety stemmed from a chemical imbalance. When I shared my concerns with her doctor, he prescribed a low dose of medication and recommended counseling. The difference we saw in her was significant. Instead of feeling tense and angry all the time, she experienced more moments of relaxation and enjoyment.

By acknowledging and addressing these emotions, we can help our children navigate their feelings with faith-based responses. Encouraging open communication, offering support, and teaching them to turn to God for strength and guidance will help them develop a strong faith and a healthy emotional understanding.

Preteens can experience intense emotions and may shut down during difficult conversations. It's important to give them time to process their feelings. Stepping away for a few minutes can help de-escalate the situation, allowing both parent and child to re-engage more calmly.

Practical Ways Faith Can Help Preteens with Anxiety

PRAYER: Teach your child to pray when they feel anxious. We will discuss this more later in the book, but prayer is a powerful tool that can provide comfort and peace. Encourage preteens to talk to God about their worries and ask for His help.

SCRIPTURE READING: Introduce your preteen to Bible verses that address anxiety and fear. Verses like Philippians 4:6–7, which encourage us not to be anxious but to present our requests to God, can be particularly comforting.

FAITH-BASED AFFIRMATIONS: Help your child create a list of affirmations based on biblical truths. Statements like "God is with me" or "I can do all things through Christ who strengthens me" can help them focus on their faith rather than their fears.

WORSHIP MUSIC: Listening to worship music can be a soothing and uplifting way to manage anxiety. Create a playlist of songs that remind them of God's love and power.

JOURNALING: Encourage your preteen to keep a faith journal where they can write down their prayers, Bible verses, and reflections on how God is helping them through their anxiety.

SERVICE: Getting involved in helping others can shift preteens' focus from their own worries to the needs of others. Volunteering or participating in church activities can provide a sense of purpose and community.

BREATHING EXERCISES: Teach them to combine breathing exercises with meditation on Scripture. For example, they can breathe in deeply while thinking of a comforting verse and breathe out slowly while letting go of their worries.

Talking to a Faith Mentor: Sometimes, talking to a trusted adult or mentor in their faith community can provide additional support and perspective. Encourage your child to build relationships with positive role models who can guide them in their faith journey.

By integrating these practical faith-based strategies, we can help our preteens manage their anxiety and strengthen their relationship with God. This approach not only addresses their immediate emotional needs but also builds a foundation for lifelong faith and resilience.

PRESSURES

Tricia

Preteens often struggle with issues of self-identity, as they begin to question who they are and where they fit in the world. This period can be marked by a heightened sense of self-consciousness and insecurity. They may struggle with body image issues, comparing themselves to peers and societal standards that can feel impossible to meet. During this time, it's essential for parents to reinforce a positive self-image and remind their children that they are wonderfully made by God.

One common struggle is the pressure to conform. Preteens may feel a strong urge to fit in with their peers, which can lead to internal conflicts between their values and the desire for acceptance. This can result in experimenting with behaviors or attitudes that are out of character. Parents can help by fostering an environment where individuality is celebrated. If your preteen wants to wear hoodies all year around—or wear bright pink lipstick and cat earrings with everything—know that these styles choice probably won't last forever. Allowing creativity and a safe space for children to express themselves without fear of judgment is important. Yet equally important is helping preteens understand the standards of caring for others. We can express ourselves with fun or interesting clothing styles, but we should not emulate bad attitudes or behaviors, even if that's what we see others doing.

Academic pressure is another significant challenge. As schoolwork becomes more demanding, preteens may experience stress and anxiety about their performance and future prospects. Encouraging a healthy balance between school and leisure activities, and emphasizing the importance of effort over perfection, can help alleviate some of this pressure. Parents should remind their children that their worth is not defined by their academic achievements, but by their character and relationship with God.

PEER INFLUENCE

Leslie

In a report published by Barna Research,[8] engaged Christian parents identified their top parenting struggles for their six- to twelve-year-olds. The list, in order from top to bottom, included peer influence, digital content, video games, busyness, social media, family struggles, and internet searches for inappropriate material.

Peer influence on a preteen's life can be significant. This is the time when our children start to figure out their own identity, think more complex thoughts, and become more aware of the world around them. Good friends can positively impact your preteen's behavior and outlook. Conversely, preteens are very susceptible to negative peer pressure and highly sensitive to the emotional impact of rejection or being left out, so poor friend choices can leave them broken-hearted and insecure.

As parents wanting to instill a faith that sticks, it's important to be aware of the friends your preteen is gravitating toward. Have conversations with them about how they should choose friends. (The book of Proverbs offers many principles to assist with this!) Help them understand the impact their choice of friends will have on them. Then, get to know your children's friends as much as possible.

When our kids were younger, David and I committed to having an open-door policy at our home and making it a fun place to hang out. That strategy paid off as we got to know our children's friends and were privileged to build lasting relationships with them. My self-proclaimed "second son" started hanging out at our house in seventh grade and remains an integral part of our family even now that he's an adult and married. I was thrilled when he randomly dropped by for dinner recently when his wife was out of town.

By taking the time to talk to your children about their choice of friends and knowing the friends they choose, you can help them navigate and make sense of the hurts, disappointments, or frustrations they're likely to experience. You'll also lay a foundation of understanding and love in your maturing relationship with your child that can hold strong even when your child moves into the teen years and beyond.

AROUND THE TABLE

Tricia

There is a difference between merely living under the same roof and cultivating a strong family identity. Achieving this takes time and intention. Time might seem like the easy part since parents already spend a lot of it driving their preteens to activities, helping with homework, and managing household chores. Yet, it's easy to slip into a "gotta get things done" mode and forget to focus on what truly matters.

A little bit of planning builds a solid foundation. When we make memories and start family traditions, we give preteens a sense of belonging and connection. Research supports this. Families who engage in regular routines have children with higher levels of emotional well-being and stronger family bonds. For example, more frequent family meals are associated with better nutrition, lower obesity rates, reduced risk behaviors, and improved mental health and academic outcomes for children and adolescents.[9] Another study, this one from Utah State University, highlights the emotional and social benefits of family mealtime, including decreased family conflict, improved happiness, and increased emotional connectedness. It also suggests that family meals can decrease the risk of substance use and risky behaviors among adolescents.[10]

Can you think back to family dinners around your kitchen table? Were they common or rare? Has your childhood experience been a springboard for how you want your own family to experience mealtimes, or do you find yourself falling into familiar habits?

BEING TOGETHER

Leslie

Family traditions lay a relational foundation that will give your children a real sense of stability and belonging that will last a lifetime. By setting aside times that you guard carefully, you're showing your children what's important to you. By laying everything else aside so you can be present with them in those moments, you're showing your children that *they're* important to you and you love spending time with them. You're not a mere spectator standing by.

Preteens who have that kind of a relationship with their family are not likely to try to avoid being seen with you in public. Quite the opposite is true; preteens who have strong parental and family bonds tend to be more confident because they have a strong foundation on which to stand as they explore their new identity and the realities of growing up. They tend to be more outgoing and empathetic to the needs of others, and they generally have stronger social skills. The time you spend with your children and the love you show them gives them a safety net as they navigate this new phase of their lives, and gives you a tremendous platform to parent them through it and point them to the truths found in God's Word all along the way.

Another benefit to preteens who have engaged parents is that they are much better prepared to handle anxi-ety and stress. Changing friendships, changing identities, changing bodies, and more contribute to the emotional upheaval many experience during this time. Parents have a unique opportunity to provide stability, a listening ear and understanding heart, and to direct their children to what is true.

> **You're showing your children that you love spending time with them. You're not a mere spectator standing by.**

Look for opportunities to have deep conversations with your preteen. Let them know that you empathize with what they're experiencing, listen patiently as they try to describe what they're feeling, and then counsel them with truth and strategize with them about how they can respond going forward. Taking the time to be in the moment with your child while they're struggling builds trust, strengthens your relationship, and enhances your platform for giving them a faith that sticks as they grow.

Family traditions and shared experiences are powerful tools in making preteens feel valued and connected. Whether it's a weekly game night, a special holiday ritual, or a simple tradition like reading together before bed, these activities become the anchors in their lives. They eagerly anticipate these moments, and they provide a sense of continuity and stability. Traditions need not be elaborate. They need to be consistent. Shared experiences become the stories our kids carry with them. Moreover, even though it's hard to believe, they become the foundation upon which they build their lives.

* * *

It's important to remember that each of our children are responsible for how they respond to the seeds we've planted and the truths we've taught them. We can't force them to accept them as their own. This is an area of surrender and faith for all parents. In 1 Corinthians 3:6–8 we find great hope for those whose children reject the faith. In that passage, we discover that Paul planted the seeds of the gospel and Apollos watered them, but it was God who caused the growth of those seeds after they took root.

As parents, we are responsible to give our children every opportunity to know God and to understand the good news found in the truths of His Word. Though we can't force our children to follow those truths or our example, we can faithfully plant and water seeds while we have the chance, and then bathe them in prayer that eventually God will cause those seeds of truth to grow into a faith that sticks.

We pray this book gives you a lot of insight into how to plant those seeds as your children grow and mature.

Part Two

COMPONENTS TO BUILDING FAITH THAT STICKS

PRAYER

BIBLE READING

CONVERSATION

SERVICE

RELATIONSHIPS

As You Build a Legacy

TO LEAVE A LASTING IMPRESSION

In Part One, we talked about the challenges of raising preteens: children who are experiencing significant changes in a world that has changed significantly since we were preteens.

Yet despite the challenges, there is so much we can do as parents to make a positive impact. Parenting preteens is hard enough, yet the current times demand even more from us. But here's the good news: We can help our children navigate these turbulent years successfully with the right tools and strategies. When we focus on these five areas of discipleship—prayer, Bible reading, conversation, service, and relationships—they'll discover how to face the challenges with the support of their parents and, even more importantly, with God.

Your active role in guiding your children in prayer and Bible reading will build habits that will direct their thoughts and help grow their relationship with God. Your discipleship in leading your children to connect through conversation, to serve others, and to build positive relationships will impact every part of their lives. Taking time to invest in these five areas is a gift now and for the future.

These five real-life ways of discipling our preteens are not new. Faithful teachers have been providing guidance on spiritual disciples for generations. And now it's our turn. This is our opportunity to place our imprint on the wet concrete of our children's hearts in order to leave a lasting impression.

Of course, many of us don't like the word "discipline." It sounds stiff. Not fun. Yet discipline simply means "learning and training." Anytime we learn something new, there will be a period of adjustment.

Spiritual disciplines are simply habits. We likely don't remember the exact moment we realized we needed to brush our teeth for our own good, instead of our mom telling us to. Yet somewhere along the way we picked up that habit so it's just what we do now. These real-life ways of discipleship we'll discuss can become the same thing. Soon it will become second nature for our kids to read their Bible, to turn to God in prayer, and to connect and care for others. They'll become habits, making God's ways known to our kids. As Psalm 16:11 says, "You make known to me the path of life; you will fill me with joy in your presence, with eternal pleasures at your right hand."

1. These habits will put our children on the right path to God.

2. These habits will draw our children to God.

3. These habits will give our children joy.

4. These habits will prepare our children for eternity with God.

This is what we want for our children. Your support and guidance will be instrumental in helping your preteens build a strong sense of self to confidently face the challenges of the preteen years and beyond.

Now let's get into the five real-life ways to build faith that sticks!

Chapter Four

FUEL THE FIRE

Why Prayer Is the Lifeblood of a Preteen's Faith

We will face moments when we feel abandoned or let down by others, but God is always steadfast. Teaching our children this truth is crucial. They need to know that while human relationships can falter, God's love and presence are unwavering. And that we have access to our loving God through prayer.

THE UNFAILING PROMISE

Leslie

As a little girl growing up in the early '80s, I cherished the simple joys of walking to school, stopping by my great-aunt's house to make sugar cookies, and being part of a close-knit community in eastern Kentucky. Our school playground was a haven of excitement, with metal slides, a fast-spinning merry-go-round, a towering jungle gym, and my favorite—the seesaw. Recess was often spent happily going up and down with my best friend, Amy.

One afternoon, a lesson came my way via the seesaw. As Amy and I enjoyed our time, our teacher called sharply, "Amy, come here!" Panicking, Amy jumped off the seesaw, leaving me to plummet to the ground. The fall scared me and knocked the wind out of me, but after recovering, I was eager to get back on.

While not a traumatizing occurrence, it was clear to me that day that people will fail me. But as I grew in Christ over the years, I learned that God will never fail us. Prayer helps preteens develop a personal relationship with God. It teaches them to turn to Him in every situation, fostering a habit of reliance on His guidance and comfort. In Hebrews 13:5, we're reminded of God's promise: "Never will I leave you; never will I forsake you." This promise is a cornerstone for Christian parents.

Memorize and recite other verses together too, like Hebrews 13:5, Jeremiah 29:11, and Romans 8:28. Discuss their meanings and how they apply to everyday situations, helping your children build a strong biblical foundation. Integrating Scripture with prayer helps them see the Bible as a living, relevant guide.

Praying with your children can profoundly influence your parenting and their development.

When my children were young, I started praying Scripture strategically for them. As they grew and I matured, I started noticing how God was answering my prayers in their lives, and I also noticed that, as I was praying God's will for them through His Word, I had more confidence in my parenting of them. God has given us a parenting manual in His Word, and we get the privilege of praying it for them and watching in awe as He directs our decisions and ideas as parents in accordance with those prayers.

Prayer is one of the most impactful practices in a child's life. Praying with your children and for them, using Scripture, can profoundly influence your parenting and their development. Teaching them to pray and seeing God's Word come alive can lay a solid foundation for their faith.

Prayer is our direct line to God, our source of strength, comfort, and guidance. It's how we communicate with the One who will never leave us nor forsake us. By integrating prayer into our family life, we model this vital connection to our children, showing them that they can always turn to God, no matter the circumstance.

INCORPORATE PRAYER INTO FAMILY LIFE
Leslie

Prayer isn't just a good habit. It's a way to build deeper connections and fortify family bonds. Having your family pray together daily can significantly impact your preteen's faith journey.

It's helpful to establish regular family prayer times. This practice fosters a deep sense of God's presence in your home. Encourage your children to voice their concerns, joys, and hopes to God, reinforcing that He listens and cares. Praying together strengthens family bonds and builds a spiritual foundation.

Setting aside time to bring your requests before God together shows your children where your faith truly lies. It also gives you opportunities to give them insights into the ways God is working within your family. Praying together about specific things your family is dealing with strengthens your relationships with one another and gives each family member a sense of belonging. At the same time, this practice will strengthen their faith in God to provide for them and walk beside them both as an individual and as a family member.

Praying together strengthens relationships and gives each family member a sense of belonging.

Maybe your spouse has a work schedule that makes it difficult to gather regularly for prayer. Or your spouse might not be a believer or hasn't found praying together to be a priority. It could be that your spouse isn't in your home at all. In cases such as these, you'll need to get creative. For example, could the family linger at the table after the meal for a brief time of prayer? Or is it possible to prioritize a few minutes before bedtime to talk about your day and pray together as a family? When you are asking God for direction and solutions, He will often give you ideas to overcome even the most difficult obstacles.

Use life's challenges as teaching moments. When setbacks occur and your preteens have struggles, guide your children to see these as opportunities to lean on God. Share how you've navigated similar situations with faith, demonstrating resilience and hope. Through prayer, they can find peace and strength in God's promises. Praying with preteens is a unique way to connect with them deeply. It shows them that their worries and joys are important to us and to God.

By leaning into His promises and teaching our children to do the same through prayer, we build a legacy of faith that will sustain them for a lifetime. Prayer is not just a ritual, it's a lifeline—a direct connection to the One who loves us unconditionally. Embrace it, model it, and instill it in your children's hearts.

A seesaw does not remain stationary but goes up and down. People also have ups and downs, and even the closest of friends may fail us. But God's love is a constant source of strength and hope. Let's guide our children to find their anchor in Him through prayer, equipping them with a faith that endures through every high and low.

MODEL DEPENDENCE ON GOD

Tricia

Leslie and I are moms in two different families, each unique in its own way. However, we both found that prayer is a powerful way to connect with God and strengthen our family relationships. We know from experience that prayer can bring us peace, healing, and strength during hard times. And we teach our kids this by showing them the power of prayer too. But first we need to be aware of what's happening in our preteen's life and then offer to pray with them.

If we know what our friend on the other side of the country ate for dinner (thank you, social media!) but are unaware of our child's struggle with a friend at school, then we have a problem. If we are quick to meet with a fellow church member who needs prayer but are too busy to stop and pray with our kids before they take a test for school, then we have a problem. If we know more about the hardships of the characters on our favorite TV show than the needs of our preteens, then we have a problem.

It's crucial to be mindful of our priorities and ensure that we are present for our children, recognizing and addressing their needs. When the need arises, stopping to pray for our children is vital. This act of pausing to bring their concerns before God not only shows them the importance of prayer but also reinforces the idea that they can always turn to God in times of need. By doing this, we teach our children that prayer is not just a routine but a powerful and immediate response to life's challenges.

We can also ask our children to pray for *us.* When we walk in faith and follow God, we are often led to numerous challenges. Seeking prayer from our preteens models how we turn to God in prayer and trust His guidance and strength.

Prayer Is a Verb

Pay attention when God breaks your heart. He's inviting you to join Him in prayer and action. Be aware of the people He brings into your life. We never know how our prayers will impact our children's lives. For example, Corrie ten Boom's family prayed for the Jewish people for decades. Long before Corrie was born, her grandfather and father felt called to hold weekly prayer meetings. Corrie grew up praying for God's chosen people, and this spiritually prepared her family to hide Jews in their home during World War II. This practice of prayer, established long before the crisis, guided their actions when the time came.

Though the situation hadn't changed, my spirit was at peace, knowing that God would follow through on His promise.

In our family, being involved in a pregnancy care center seemed like it took away from typical homeschooling activities. I was one of three founding members who started a pregnancy care center in our community. This commitment meant juggling various responsibilities, but it also provided invaluable lessons in faith and prayer for my children.

We often prayed for the center's needs, whether it was for volunteers, financial support, or resources for the mothers we were helping. Time and again, we saw God provide in miraculous ways. These experiences left a lasting impression on my children. They witnessed firsthand how powerful and effective prayer could be.

When my oldest daughter, Leslie Joy, needed funds to become a missionary, she recalled those prayers and God's provision for the center. This memory bolstered her faith and determination. She knew that if God could provide for the center, He could also provide for her missionary journey. And He did, in ways that were beyond our imagination.

I asked my daughter Leslie Joy to share what happened when she found out she needed to prove she had all the mandatory funds for her yearlong stay as a missionary before she could be granted a visa.

Leslie Joy relayed:

My heart sank. I had no idea that this was a requirement, and I didn't have the money. I had only a few hundred dollars in my account, with a bit more pledged. Where would I get the thousands of dollars required?

"God, I know You promised You will provide," I prayed. "Please show me how this should happen." After the prayer, I felt a shift in my heart. Though the situation hadn't changed, my spirit was at peace, knowing that God would follow through on His promise.

About ten minutes later, I was reading through my email again and felt nudged to check my spam box. I opened it, and inside was a notification from PayPal: a donation that covered all the money I needed had come through the link I'd posted on my blog (which, by the way, didn't reveal the amount of money I needed). Everything, all at once! And the most incredible part? It had come through about half an hour before I even knew I needed it.

A friend I hadn't seen in more than five years made the donation. When I contacted him and asked what inspired him to send it, he said, "I just want you to know you were a big part of God's plan in my life to know Christ as my Savior. And I hope you will let God use you so lots of others will know Christ."

Leslie Joy saw us serve others through the pregnancy center and turn to God to do so, praying for every need. We had lived out lives of faith and prayer, and when she faced challenges, she followed what she'd seen modeled: turning to God in prayer.

Living out our faith together as a family is a powerful way to instill lasting beliefs in our children. When they see us relying on God's promises and turning to Him in prayer, they learn to do the same.

Inviting God's Presence

Prayer is not a one-size-fits-all practice, but finding what works for your family can be life-changing. By prioritizing prayer, we invite God to change us and to work in and through us.

You and I can't become better people by finding the right recipe for prayer or checking off a list of spiritual disciplines. We can't manufacture understanding or compassion for others by willpower. We can't produce the fruit of the Spirit by rolling up our sleeves. We best experience love, joy, peace, patience, kindness, goodness, faithfulness, gentleness, and self-control when we grant the Holy Spirit access to every part of our hearts. If anything should be on our to-do list, it's this: Connect with Jesus through prayer. Fall more deeply in love with Him. Depend on Him more in real and active ways.

PRAYER IN ALL THINGS

Leslie

Praying Through Family Difficulties

For the last twelve years, our family has led a ministry to home-school families called Teach Them Diligently. The road has not always been easy. Our faith has been tried. Finances have been tight, and some people have been hurtful. David and I vowed from the beginning that we wouldn't hide these realities from our children.

Although we were careful to never lay more on them than they needed to know, we were able to engage them in our prayers that God would bring in the families who needed to be at our events, that He would work in their lives and strengthen them through what they learned while they were there.

We prayed together that God would meet our needs and allow us to continue to do the work He had called us to do. We rejoiced to-gether over the testimonies that came in, and we prayed together when it looked like the hurdles in front of us were too high for us to scale. Our children were able to see God's hand in what we considered good things, and they were able to see God's hand in our trials as well. They were able to watch David and me as we modeled a life of faith for them and, through it all, the God who upheld our family during their child-hood has become the God they seek with their own issues now.

Involve your children in praying about family matters. When you share your struggles and pray together, especially as your preteens desire to be more mature, you build trust and deepen their faith. My children grew up praying for various challenges we faced, including those related to homeschooling and community outreach. By involving them in these prayers, they developed a habit of turning to prayer as their first response to difficulties. This habit will serve them well throughout their lives.

Teaching Moments Through Prayer Times Together

We've already talked about how intensely preteens can feel their emotions. As they're starting to become more empathetic, they may intensely feel the pain of one of their friend's struggles. Often they may be confused or overwhelmed by what they're trying to express. Praying together, helping them understand that they can trust you, and even more importantly, they can trust God with their requests and their struggles, is a great privilege.

Those who are striving to parent biblically and who have been bathing their children in prayer personally will often find that as they are praying, God's Word will flow out of them in their children's hearing. Through our prayers, we have the opportunity to speak truths to them as we pray those truths to God. Presenting truth in this manner is a powerful way to teach our children to think biblically. God uses parents in amazing ways to point our children to Him.

Guilt Trips and Sensitive Children

As our preteens are figuring things out, they may be quick to blame themselves for everything, causing parents to wrestle with how to help them understand grace while also helping them keep a right perspective about sin. Children at this age are starting to understand how their actions impact others, which can be a two-edged sword because it often makes it difficult for them to forgive themselves for what they've done or to accept the grace that's offered them through the forgiveness of others.

Once again, parents can see the power of praying together to teach their children valuable truths as they're able to pray in accordance with the truths of Scripture. First John 1:9 reminds us that if we confess our sins, Jesus is faithful to forgive us. We can thank God that He removes our sins from us as far as the east is from the west as we read in Psalm 103:12, and we can thank God that there is now no condemnation for those who are in Christ Jesus.

We can pray that we can take our thoughts captive and make them obedient to Christ as we see in 2 Corinthians 10:5, and we can help them better understand the freedom and restoration found in Christ alone. We're also showing them that God cares about them in their struggles. He has given them countless proofs of that in Scripture, and we want them to see it in their own lives as well.

With Thanksgiving

Instilling a sense of gratitude and thanksgiving in our children is not only a spiritual discipline, but it will be positively impactful for their health, emotional well-being, and more as they continue to grow. Together, you can look for things to be grateful for and make a point to thank God for them together. Rejoice over the goodness He shows you. Be intentional about praying with thanksgiving. It will change the way you and your children look at the world around you.

Prayer Makes a Difference

Including your children in your prayer life and allowing them to witness how God answers prayers can have a profound impact. The power of prayer can transform not only individual lives but also family dynamics. Sharing stories of answered prayers, like that of Corrie ten Boom, helps illustrate the long-term effects of a faithful prayer life.

Prayer is one of the critical aspects of a child's development. By making it a daily practice, we instill values and habits that will stay with them for life. Remember, it's not just about praying for their immediate needs but about building a relationship with God that will guide them through all stages of life.

By prioritizing prayer, we provide our children with a strong foundation of faith and resilience, preparing them to face the future with confidence and trust in God. And we can guide our children in making it a reflex—which basically means turning to prayer first.

When children are young, it's easy to pray with them about the little things, but it's important that we keep that habit alive as they become preteens.

Philippians 4:6–7 tells us not to be anxious about anything. Rather, we're told to take our requests to God. When children are young, it's easy to pray with them about the little things, but it's important that we keep that habit alive as they become preteens. We want to set them on a course where their knee-jerk reaction or reflex is to take every request, every concern, every care, and every want to the God who can provide and answer.

"Let's stop and pray about that now" has been a regular statement around our home for as long as I can remember.

Big or small, important or insignificant, we make it a point to take our requests to God. It's been exciting to watch as our kids started adopting that policy on their own, often surprising their friends by asking to stop and pray with them about whatever their friend was struggling with. That reflex of taking their cares to God is foundational for building a faith that sticks.

Making prayer a regular part of life instills a natural response to various situations. It becomes second nature to pray for an ambulance when you see one, or for someone who is sick. This reflexive prayer habit is what we aim to cultivate in our children.

* * *

When we model and instill the habit of prayer in our children, we are equipping them with a powerful tool for life. Prayer becomes their first response, not their last resort. In a world full of distractions, it is easy to lose sight of what truly matters. However, by prioritizing prayer and making it a natural part of our daily routine, we help our children develop a strong, enduring faith. This faith will guide them through the challenges of life, providing comfort and direction.

Let's commit to stopping and praying with our children, teaching them to seek God in all circumstances. In doing so, we not only strengthen their faith but also build a legacy of trust and dependence on God that will carry them through all the seasons of their lives.

Chapter Five

THE ULTIMATE GUIDEBOOK

Why Reading the Bible Is Essential in Your Preteen's Life

The most important thing about reading our Bible with our preteens is . . . just reading. We can trust that God will give us the wisdom we need. We shouldn't worry about having all the answers. Instead, we can seek out answers with our preteens. In fact, they'll probably learn more that way!

A HUNGER FOR THE WORD OF GOD

Tricia

I was barely getting my life together when I became a mom. Seventeen when I had my son, I prayed that I could raise him differently than I had been raised and that he would know God from an early age. I did not know my biological dad growing up, and my stepdad was not a Christian. However, my mom became a believer when I was around eight years old. She was a new believer, and things did not really change much at home during the week. She would still watch the same types of movies she did before and listen to the same type of music, but then, on Sundays, she would be on her knees at the altar praying that she would do things differently.

Since my mom hadn't been raised in a Christian home, her faith walk was two steps forward and one step back, but even though that was the case, I took a few things to heart: the church was necessary, and the people at church really cared for our family. More than that, God loved me. Even though I wanted to do things my own way during my teen years, deep down, I believed in Jesus.

My stepdad's faith was nonexistent, and my mom's faith was new, but attending church and being surrounded by loving believers made an impact. I watched how they worshiped God and read their Bible. I felt their love. Then, when I felt abandoned and alone—forgotten by my former boyfriend and friends as a pregnant teen—the seeds of faith that had been planted as a preteen took root. Six months pregnant, I trusted that Jesus loved me and had good plans for me. The day I confessed my sins and ask Him to be my Savior, I also opened up my Bible and started reading. Having the Spirit within, the words became alive to me. I wish I could say that I developed a regular Bible reading habit at that time, but I didn't.

As a single mom, I prayed for a future husband. I prayed for someone who would love God, love me, and love my son, and God answered that prayer with John. John's growing-up years were utterly different from mine. His parents were Christians, and he had been taught about God his whole life. One of his favorite memories was the summer he was in elementary school and his mom read through the Bible with him and his siblings, explaining it as she read. He says he learned more about the Bible that summer than in all his years in the church. Later, John's dad became a pastor. In fact, that's how I met John. My mom and I attended his parents' church.

John and I came from two completely different backgrounds, yet together we led and guided our kids. And while there were times when we read our Bibles together, everything changed in my spiritual life when I developed consistency with my own Bible reading.

Making the Bible a Priority

As a young mom, I made a decision to read the Bible every morning. John and I lived in a 600-square-foot apartment. Our oldest son, Cory, was three years old, and I had a newborn baby girl, Leslie Joy. John was in college, and he delivered pizzas at night. We were broke. Really broke. We only had one car, so I was home with the kids all day and we had no television. I don't remember what gave me the desire, but I was determined to wake up before my kids every day to read the Bible. So I set an alarm clock to get up early. Then I placed that clock across the room. I knew that would force me to jump out of bed and turn off the alarm before it woke the kids. I don't think that habit lasted long, probably because I was exhausted. And probably because, while I was well-meaning, the time seemed more like an obligation rather than a joy. Maybe you can relate! Perhaps you're in a season where you have allowed the busyness of life to push Bible reading and study to the side. Or maybe it's sheer exhaustion that's kept you from spending time in God's Word.

Thankfully, a couple of years later, I was able to spend time nearly every morning in God's Word. It became a habit. When my kids were preteens, they'd emerge from their bedroom to find me reading my Bible on the sofa. Or they'd find me and John reading together. Soon they developed their own Bible reading habits.

At the time I didn't understand how much my example was impacting my children. Now that my oldest children are adults, regular Bible reading has become a habit for them, and they often share what they'd been reading with others. I was especially thrilled when I learned that two of my adult children were reading and studying the same passages and meeting to discuss what they'd learned, even though they lived thousands of miles apart. My desire to make the Bible a priority has led to my children desiring to make the Bible a priority in their lives too.

Doable Daily Practices

We say that God's Word is life. But do we really believe it? The truth is that often we sit down with our Bibles to read because of obligation, but let's think about that. In our attempts at perseverance and dedication, devotion can sometimes turn into duty, leading to a dull experience. Gradually, we become apathetic, and our daily reading becomes another checklist item rather than an opportunity to know and adore the God of the universe.

If you've been in church for any amount of time, you've probably heard about the importance of building a habit of Bible reading. While it's important to set aside time, we should never see reading God's Word as just another task. Like almost everything else, our preteens learn how to read God's Word by watching us do it. Here are daily practices we can start, model, and then teach.

ASK GOD TO GIVE YOU A HUNGER FOR HIS WORD. It's a crucial first step. Is Bible reading hard for you? Admit it. Pray, "Jesus, something is off here. I want to know You, the living God, more deeply and commune with You through Your Word rather than just checking off a box. Give me a desire for Your Word." This desire for genuine connection moves us from obligation to adoration. As you stick with it, you'll find duty transforming into heartfelt dialogue. He loves to meet us and delights in seeing us faithfully pursue Him.

INVITE THE HOLY SPIRIT TO JOIN IN YOUR READING. Start by asking the Holy Spirit to speak to your heart. Acknowledge when it feels hard and dry. Ask for a new hunger for His Word. Don't be afraid to change your routine or ask for help to see old words with new eyes. Through our example we can show preteens how the Holy Spirit teaches us and helps us remember what Jesus taught. The Bible is living and active by the Holy Spirit's power.

PLAN TO DO WHAT YOU READ. Sit down with your Bible, intending to take God's Word seriously and live it out. Ask, "How can I be living and active with Your Word?"

READ THE EXCITING PARTS. Consider reading parts of the Bible you've rarely read before. For example, in 1 Samuel 27, David, fearing for his life, seeks refuge in Philistine territory and becomes a servant of King Achish. In 1 Samuel 28, Saul, desperate for guidance, visits a medium to summon the spirit of the deceased prophet Samuel. Despite this turmoil, Psalm 56 shows David's heart—trusting in God despite difficult circumstances. Nothing boring about that, right?

WHISPER PRAYERS OF ADORATION BEFORE YOU READ. Turn to God with a heart of adoration. A simple prayer is, "Lord, You are amazing. Help me see that today—in Your Word and every part of my life." This transforms obligation into vibrant adoration, opening our eyes, minds, and hearts to every moment in our lives.

Bible Reading as a Family

Reading the Bible together as a family can greatly impact a preteen's faith journey. It can help families stay close to their faith and build a strong foundation. We know it can be hard to find the right way to do things, but families can make Bible reading interesting and relevant for their preteens by using age-appropriate reading plans and discussion topics.

Ultimately, the goal is to find a way to read the Bible together as a family that works. (We will share more ideas for Bible reading time with preteens in the next chapter.) There isn't one right way or wrong way to read your Bible with preteens. Families can be open and flexible in how they do things. Don't overcomplicate this or approach it in a way that's not sustainable for you. Consistency is more important than perfection. The point isn't to check off chapters. The point is understanding the truth of God's Word and learning to apply it in our everyday lives.

Start Simple: Just Read

Sometimes, when we consider what will help us raise men and women of faith, we think it needs to be complicated—that we should have lessons planned or topics to discuss. Or we worry that we're not up to the challenge. The good news is that God's Word is living and active. We can trust that simply reading it together will have a profound impact. It's not about having all the answers, but about the journey of seeking those answers together. This approach not only helps our preteens learn but also strengthens our own faith as we grow alongside them.

The simplicity of opening the Bible, dedicating time to read, and being open to discussing and discovering together is powerful.

As was the case for John's mom, sometimes the most ordinary things are those that matter most in the long run. It wasn't tricky for Darlyne to open her Bible and read to her kids. It required time, a Bible, and a willingness to read and to answer questions. Some answers she knew. Other answers she didn't.

The simplicity of opening the Bible, dedicating time to read, and being open to discussing and discovering together is powerful. It's these moments of shared exploration and learning that will shape their faith and ours.

SETTING THE EXAMPLE

Leslie

I became a Christian when I was young and, by God's grace, I did not go through times of doubt. While I certainly wasn't perfect, my faith in God and trust in His love for me as His child remained secure. As a teenager, I committed to studying His Word and praying every day. I have journals filled with notes and prayers from that time, providing a detailed look into my spiritual growth.

My husband, David, has a different testimony. He started attending church at age eight, picked up by the church bus, initially motivated by the prospect of winning a prize. Shortly after, he invited his parents to join him, and eventually, both his mom and dad came to know the Lord. Although David's father passed away when he was ten, his mom made sure David stayed in church through his teen years. Despite having extensive head knowledge from Sunday school, David didn't put his faith in God until he was twenty-four. When he did, his zeal and desire to grow in his faith were incredible, and he began devouring God's Word whenever he could.

By the time David and I married and had children, both of us had the habit of starting our day with the Lord. When our children woke up in the morning, the first thing they saw was Mom and Dad spending time with Him. We didn't realize then how powerful it was to model our faith in action this way.

We were whetting their appetite for God's Word and modeling how to start the day.

I've often prayed Scripture for my children, and God frequently answered those prayers through simple ideas I'd come up with. When the children were young, I would talk to them about what God taught me in my devotions, or something I was praying about while we sat at breakfast. The consistency of my sharing (and David's, when he could join us) led to their desire to read their Bibles and share with us what they were learning. By the time they were preteens, our breakfast conversations had grown lengthy as we discussed together various things we read, thought about, or prayed about.

In hindsight, I realized that David and I were whetting their appetite for God's Word and modeling how to start the day. Since David and I were the only Christians our children saw in the early mornings, they assumed all Christians began their day with devotions and discussions.

I'm so grateful for what God has done with that. My children, having grown up with this morning rhythm, formed their own habits of Bible study and prayer early on. As we shared what we were learning, my kids are now unbelievably bold in talking about their faith. By following God's answer to our prayer that our children would know His Word, we set an example of personal Bible reading that has stayed with them through the years.

Laying a Foundation

In the evenings, we often read the Bible aloud together and prayed about things that were important to each of us. Using a curriculum or plan rarely worked well for us. Instead, we found that merely reading a passage of Scripture aloud and discussing it was the best fit. Sometimes David or I would read, and sometimes the kids would, but it was unfailingly interesting to hear how each individual often got something slightly different from the same passage.

Since God's Word is alive and personal, and the Holy Spirit is at work in the lives of His children, this evening Bible reading and sharing reinforced for my kids the personal nature of our great God. This time in the evening was just the icing on the cake after a day spent discussing things of God and teaching our children diligently as we went through the mundane activities of our day, as Deuteronomy 6 instructs us to do.

There have been several times through the years that our evening Bible times have been derailed by a mispronounced word—or just a lot of silliness that breaks out because kids are tired and giggly. I saw a video recently of my boys imitating an old evangelist they used to hear on the radio each evening as they went to sleep. They read Psalm 1 modeling his voice and expression. We laughed till we cried, and although I wouldn't call that evening a serious time in God's Word, it was beneficial. To this day, when any of us comes across Psalm 1, we read it in that voice. It has become part of the tapestry that makes our family unique, and I wouldn't trade it for the world.

By setting the example through our daily habits and intentional conversations, we've fostered a deep and enduring faith in our children. Our consistent devotion times, both morning and evening, coupled with open discussions about God's Word, has laid a strong foundation for their spiritual growth and boldness in sharing their faith.

Sharing What You Learn

It's not just those morning times that provide significant moments around God's Word. Sharing what God is teaching you and discovering what God is teaching your children introduces a dependency on His Word and gives you insight into their hearts and minds.

Our family has homeschooled for years, and God often gives us concrete examples to reinforce what we've been learning together. We'll be reading the Bible or studying a related topic, and within a day or two, a real-life situation perfectly reflects what we just learned.

However you educate your children, you can be intentional and seize these moments. You can say, "Remember that passage we read in the Bible? See how it applies here?" This makes their faith tangible and memorable. Parenting preteens gives us countless opportunities to make these connections. We're with them every day, doing life together. This constant interaction allows us to weave their Bible studies into their daily experiences, showing them how their faith applies to real-world situations. It's a truly effective way to raise our children in a faith that will stick.

Throughout our lives, God has taught David and me lessons we wish we had learned years ago. Since discipleship involves leveraging what we're learning for the good of others, we've been intentional about sharing those lessons to help our children learn them much sooner than we did. And we don't worry about how they might react to what we're sharing. Sometimes things get uncomfortable, but these are still things that are important to talk about.

David's testimony is very different from mine. He was an alcoholic before he came to know the Lord, and when God got his attention, his life changed drastically. As we've spent time together talking about things God has taught us, our children have become active participants in that. It's an amazing thing to be able to grow closer to the Lord with your children growing right along with you.

By not worrying about their possible reaction, giving context to what you learn each day, and sharing what you learn, we can instill a deep, enduring faith in our children. These practices help them see the relevance of God's Word in everyday life and develop a personal relationship with Him that will last a lifetime.

A TIME OF TRANSITION

Tricia

While it's important to help preteens engage with Bible reading, remember that this is just one of many challenges they are facing. Preteens are in a time of significant transition, and they may feel overwhelmed by the number of changes happening. It's easy to forget that, despite their growing independence and maturity, they are still the same little kids on the inside.

I confess that I've made the mistake of expecting too much too soon. The physical changes they undergo can make it seem like they're ready for more responsibility and greater challenges. However, their emotional and mental development might not be keeping pace with their physical growth.

BALANCE YOUR EXPECTATIONS WITH PATIENCE AND UNDERSTANDING. Encourage them to take on new responsibilities, but also allow them the space to be kids. Celebrate their progress, no matter how small, and provide support when they struggle.

REMEMBER TO COMMUNICATE OPENLY WITH YOUR PRETEEN. Let them know that you don't understand everything about the

Bible either. It's okay to admit that you also have questions and that sometimes, life gets so busy that even you miss days of Bible reading. Share with them that hard times can bring new questions and challenges in your faith.

TELL THEM YOU DON'T EXPECT THEM TO BE PERFECT. Reassure them that it's normal to have ups and downs in their spiritual journey. Encourage them to keep trying and remind them that growth takes time.

By recognizing the challenges they face and offering a supportive environment, you can help your preteen develop resilience and confidence. This approach not only fosters their spiritual growth but also strengthens your relationship with them during these formative years. Here are some tips to do that well:

1. Engage with them at a heart level: Take the time to build a relationship with your preteen by sitting next to them during Bible reading, talking with them and asking their thoughts, and looking them in the eye. This can help alleviate their insecurities and create a strong foundation for communication, making Bible reading a shared and meaningful experience.

2. Use questions instead of making accusations: I wish that every session of Bible reading has been uplifting, but there are times when my kids have acted downright disrespectfully. When they seem to have a bad attitude about Bible reading, I've learned to ask questions to understand their perspective and the reasons behind their actions. There have been times our older adopted kids didn't want to read the Bible, and asking questions helped me understand why. They didn't understand how a loving God could allow bad things to happen. Have you ever wondered about that?

   Our adopted kids have been through hard things, and they

had a hard time believing that God allowed those things to happen to them. By understanding where they were coming from, I chose stories from the Bible where bad things did happen, yet God brought good through them at the end. It would have been easy just to discipline them for their bad attitudes, but by asking questions I was able to understand what was really going on. This approach can lead to deeper conversations about faith and help preteens think through their thoughts and emotions regarding Scripture.

3. Maintain consistent expectations and traditions: Despite the changes and challenges of the preteen years, keep family traditions and expectations intact, including regular Bible reading times.

4. Provide a safe and supportive environment: Preteens may feel insecure and vulnerable, so it's crucial to create a safe space where they can express themselves without judgment. Be there to listen, offer guidance, and encourage their Bible reading by pointing them toward truth.

5. Plant seeds for the future: Even if it seems like your preteen is not paying attention or is resisting Bible reading, continue to plant seeds of faith and positive habits. These seeds may take root and have a lasting impact on their lives, even if they don't fully appreciate it at the time.

✳   ✳   ✳

Remember, every child is unique, so it's important to adapt these strategies to fit your child's individual needs and personality. It's okay to try things and then readjust, because in the end it's worth the effort. After all, Bible reading is vital in a preteen's life for many reasons, both now and for the future.

By instilling the habit of Bible reading during these formative years, you are nurturing a lifelong connection to God's Word, ensuring that your preteen carries its truth and comfort into adulthood, strengthening their faith and character for years to come.

Chapter Six

DISCOVER TRUTHS TOGETHER

Practical Tips for Reading the Bible with Your Preteen

Family Bible reading doesn't have to be formulaic. Consistency is more important than perfection. Whether you're reading a psalm or a few verses from a chapter or talking about Scripture as you listen to a news story, what matters is making it a regular part of your family's routine. Engage your children by asking, "What does the Bible have to say about this?" or "What does that mean to you?" Share your insights as well.

KEEPING IT REAL

Leslie

My second son, Payton, is incredibly bright, but he's always had some "absent-minded professor" tendencies. (Or "no walking-around sense," as my father often described it.) This often showed up in school. He would make high grades on his tests but do poorly in co-op classes because he would leave his completed homework on his bed at home rather than taking it with him to turn in.

He struggled with laziness and procrastination, and as a preteen, these qualities were becoming increasingly prominent in his life. He began to notice that his actions, or lack thereof, were no longer just affecting him. These actions were also causing problems for his brother, who was his roommate, and even his younger sisters, who were often frustrated with him. Despite lectures and punishments, these tendencies persisted. So Payton and I turned to God's Word together to find the answer.

We found our lesson in a most surprising place and had a wonderful time learning a lesson neither of us will ever forget. We read Proverbs 6:6–11, which instructs us to "go to the ant," and provides many details about what we can learn from them. Knowing my little brainiac loved gathering tidbits of knowledge to impress his grandparents, I asked him to learn everything he could about ants and come back to discuss his findings. He dove into that project with enthusiasm. At eleven, he was excited to tell me these interesting ant facts:

They work tirelessly, even without a leader, to prepare their food for the winter.

They think ahead, which is why they're always prepared.

They take initiative and are self-motivated.

Army ants build living bridges by linking together when they get to an obstacle they can't cross.

There are ants who conquer other ant hills and make their captives their slaves.

Ants can become zombies.

Ants can lift ten to fifty times their body weight.

I texted him as I was writing this just to see what he still remembered from that lesson all those years ago, and he immediately started sending me pertinent details about ants, which made me smile.

We were both amazed at how God created ants, and all the interesting things we could learn from them. That time spent searching God's Word for practical lessons and connecting them to a fascinating insect left an indelible mark on both of us. It showed my eleven-year-old son that God's Word is incredibly practical, and that God's creativity is awe-inspiring.

That study also gave us something tangible to go back to when he would be slipping into his old habits again. Having that common idea to remember also lessened the tension in our relationship. Instead of a lecture about laziness and procrastination, all Payton needed to hear going forward was, "Is that what an ant would do?" The point would be made, and he'd move the project forward or take more initiative.

It was a definite win-win for me and my preteen.

Navigate Tough Topics

Navigating tough topics in the Bible—and in the world—can be challenging, but with the right approach, it can be a valuable learning experience for preteens. When difficult subjects arise, don't shy away from them. Instead, use them as opportunities to have meaningful conversations and deepen their understanding of faith.

Encourage your preteens to reflect on their day and identify situations where they can apply biblical teachings. For example, if they read about kindness in the Bible, ask them to think about moments when they were kind or when they could have shown more kindness.

Encourage your preteens to ask questions and express their thoughts and doubts. It's okay to not have all the answers.

Also discuss challenging people who seem to thrive on being unkind to others. Your preteen can most likely list off many examples. Then look to see how people in the Bible handled unkindness. For example, David refused to strike out at Saul even though Saul sought his life. If your preteen is wondering how so many bad things happen to people through no fault of their own, read from the book of Job. Seeing both the heartache and joy in this book can help us think through ideas of faith, perseverance, and trust in God. Job is someone who faced immense suffering despite being a righteous man. Talk about how Job remained faithful through his hardships, and the lessons we can learn from his unwavering trust in God.

Additionally, you can bring up other biblical figures like Joseph, who was sold into slavery by his brothers but later rose to power in Egypt. Joseph's faith and perseverance through difficult times led to a greater purpose. Or consider discussing Jesus Himself, who endured suffering and crucifixion for the salvation of humanity.

Be honest and open about the complexities and nuances of these stories. Encourage your preteens to ask questions and express their thoughts and doubts. This openness fosters a safe environment for exploration and growth. Remember, it's okay to not have all the answers, but don't allow your lack of knowledge to hold you back from having conversations with your children. Use these moments to seek answers together, whether through further Bible study, consulting faith leaders, or researching reliable sources.

Also, encourage your preteens to think critically and develop their own understanding of biblical teachings. This process builds a strong foundation for their faith, rooted in personal conviction and thoughtful reflection. Support them in their journey—with an open Bible as your guide—and remind them that questioning and seeking understanding are vital parts of spiritual growth.

GETTING DOWN TO IT

Leslie

Here are some ideas to help preteens understand and apply what they learn from reading the Bible:

JOURNALING: Encourage your preteens to keep a journal where they can write down their thoughts, questions, and reflections on their Bible readings. This practice helps them process and internalize what they read.

DISCUSSION GROUPS: Organize small group discussions with other preteens or family members. Sharing insights and perspectives can enrich their understanding and make Bible study more engaging.

CREATIVE ACTIVITIES: Incorporate activities like drawing, storytelling, or role-playing to bring biblical stories to life. These activities make learning more interactive and enjoyable.

SERVICE PROJECTS: Connect Bible teachings to community service projects. For instance, after reading about generosity, plan a family activity to help those in need. This hands-on approach reinforces the lessons and shows how faith translates into action.

BIBLE APPS AND RESOURCES: Utilize technology by exploring Bible apps and online resources designed for preteens. These tools often include interactive features, games, and videos that make Bible study more accessible and fun.[11]

Connecting preteens with the Bible requires intentionality and creativity. By making connections between Scripture and everyday life, navigating tough topics with openness, and engaging in practical and interactive activities, you can foster a deep and lasting interest in the Bible.

Embrace challenging conversations and use them as opportunities to nurture kids' faith and guide them toward a strong, resilient spiritual foundation. Through these efforts, you help your preteens grow into thoughtful, compassionate, and faithful individuals.

BRING THE BIBLE TO LIFE

Tricia

When John and I were first married, we decided to take Bible college classes offered through our church. Before we started the class, our pastor asked us to take a test so he could gauge how much we already knew. Let's just say I'm not sure I got more than a few answers right!

Even though I'd been raised going to church since I was about eight, Bible reading wasn't part of our family's everyday life. I didn't know if Abraham lived before David or where stories like Noah's ark or Samson were in the timeline. Our Sunday school classes were often taught by themes rather than a through-the-Bible approach. I had a lot to learn!

Through those Bible classes, which included reading books like *What the Bible Is All About* by Henrietta Myers, I learned about the layout of the Bible. I discovered that the books of the Bible are organized by groupings. I started to understand the types of books, like history and poetry. I'm so thankful that I had this foundation, because it's knowledge I've later been able to pass on to my kids.

Perhaps you find yourself where I was, and you feel insufficient to guide your preteens because you don't understand much yourself. The good news is that this is a perfect time to learn together. Pick up a book like *What the Bible Is All About* or find a Bible reading plan to do together. It could be reading through the whole Bible or just one book.

One of my favorite activities is reading through the Psalms with my children. We set a timer and see how much we can read together. The Psalms are filled with rich content—they tell of sin and repentance, worship, and raw human emotion. We each take turns reading a few verses at a time, and it has brought a lot of interesting conversations. I mean, how could you not have great conversations with verses like Psalm 22:6? "But I am a worm and not a man, scorned by everyone, despised by the people." That brought a lot of laughter, and it also helped us realize that David "got up in his feels" a lot—which made my kids feel better about when their emotions hijack them too! Even spending just fifteen minutes reading the Psalms can reveal so much about faith and human experience.

The more we make learning about the Bible part of everyday life, the more our preteens see that there is much to learn, discover, and apply.

Also, even more recently, my friend Michelle and I started a podcast where we read through the Bible chronologically. In the podcast we share a summary of the day's reading and also talk about how it applies to our lives. (You can check it out for yourself. Just look for the Daily Bible Podcast.) Putting on podcasts like these during drives to practices or other extracurricular activities—anytime you're in the car—is an easy way to discover the Bible in new ways.

The more we make learning about the Bible part of everyday life, the more our preteens see that there is much to learn, discover, and apply. The Bible doesn't have to be confusing, scary, or complicated. Learning a little bit about God's purpose, God's plans, and God's promises through His Word makes it simple to relate back to in everyday life.

Interactive Bible Reading

Does your preteen seem to zone out when you're reading your Bible? Then bring it to life! There is plenty of action and dialogue for family members to act out. Not only is this fun, it also helps kids "see" the Bible stories for themselves. These interactive projects help make the Bible come alive for your preteens, and they also create cherished memories.

For example, years ago for Christmas we started a tradition of assigning roles and sound effects for the Christmas story, making it fun and engaging. This is still our favorite Christmas tradition.

John prints the Christmas story from Luke with key words bolded.

We have reactions for each of those bolded words on slips of paper. Then we have family members draw them from a jar.

As the Bible story is read, everyone must pay attention. When a bolded word in the story is spoken, the reader pauses to allow the participant assigned to the word to call out their part. For instance, when the word "Jesus" is read, John pauses to allow the assigned participant to call out, "God saves." When the participant hears "Immanuel," he or she says, "God is with us." Making it more fun, when the audience hears "birth," the sound effect could be "ouchie, ouchie." Then "baby" elicits a hearty "waahhh!" This allows readers and listeners to participate in the Christmas story. It's a fun way to share the Bible story and get family members of all ages involved!

When our oldest kids were preteens, John and I led children's church. Every week, John and his friend Kenny would make the Bible come alive by writing skits for Bible stories. They'd also write application skits to show how the Bible applies to our lives, and let kids be the main actors! We loved incorporating these skits into children's church for many years, but you can also do the same at home!

Real-Life Examples to Follow

When we first brought home our adopted girls, three of them were preteens and one was a teen. While we did have Bible reading time during homeschool, I felt there was only so much I could tell them about how to apply the Bible to their lives before they started to tune me out. That's when I decided to turn to stories of men and women living out God's Word—stories filled with danger and excitement!

Incorporating real-life stories, especially those of missionaries, can greatly enhance devotional time. We love using the YWAM (Youth With A Mission) missionary books. These books provide vivid examples of faith in action, showing how missionaries overcame incredible challenges through God's strength.

For instance, Gladys Aylward, one of our favorite missionaries, exemplified incredible courage. She once walked into a prison riot where prisoners were armed with machetes and commanded them to put down their weapons—and they did. Discussing such stories allows us to tie biblical principles to real-life examples, reinforcing the message that through Christ, we can do all things.

IDEAS FOR FAMILY DEVOTIONS
Leslie

Creating a routine for family devotions can be a powerful way to grow together in faith. Here are some more examples to inspire and guide your family time:

READ A PSALM TOGETHER EACH NIGHT. Psalms are rich in emotion and wisdom, providing a perfect starting point for family discussions and reflections.

READ ONE CHAPTER A NIGHT. Just reading one chapter a night can help your family journey through the New Testament in nine or ten months, or the entire Bible in about three-and-a-half years. This steady, manageable pace helps build a consistent habit of Bible reading.

BOOK STUDIES. As our children grew older, we dove into books like James and Philippians, extracting deeper lessons and applying them to our lives. These studies fostered more profound conversations and understanding.

DEVOTIONALS. There are fantastic devotional books available that cater to all ages and stages. These can facilitate meaningful conversations around God's Word, making it relevant and accessible for everyone.

WRITING SCRIPTURE. A great way to help both you and your children pay attention to what you're reading is by writing Scripture in a journal. This practice encourages reflection and application while sneaking in some handwriting practice! In my personal devotions, I've journaled through most of the New Testament this way, and my children have worked through James and Philippians with me.

By incorporating these methods, you can create a rich and engaging environment for your family's spiritual growth. Each approach offers a unique way to connect with God's Word, making family devotions a cherished and transformative experience.

* * *

By reading the Bible together as a family, you're not only teaching your children about God's Word but also fostering a habit of personal Bible reading. Engaging in these practices while they are young helps them see the Bible as a source of daily nourishment and joy. This habit becomes a foundational aspect of their lives, guiding them as they grow older.

Encouraging your children to develop their own devotional habits can be incredibly rewarding. As we have shared, the impact of these practices can be seen as our children grow. Building good habits and instilling a reflex of turning to God's Word equips them with the spiritual tools they need for the future.

Chapter Seven

TALK ABOUT ANYTHING AND EVERYTHING

Making Deep Connections

Spending time talking with your preteen is vital for their development and for building family bonds. Conversations with parents provide a space for preteens to hone communication skills, practice active listening, and clearly express themselves. This builds confidence and reduces insecurities common among peers. It also equips them to better connect with people of all ages.

THE GIFT OF BEING PRESENT

Leslie

Recently I had the opportunity to spend the entire day with my ten- and eleven-year-old nephews. It was a blast from start to finish! We started with a culinary adventure as I introduced them to meatball subs. Then, we played a few games of Taco Cat Goat Cheese Pizza. Finally, feeling fueled and ready for a challenge, we hiked to a nearby waterfall. I had a great time, and I think they did too.

As we hiked up the steep path, they talked almost the entire time. I learned about their friends, their new classes, their neighbor's dog, the connection between Halifax and the *Titanic*, a camp that has special days they get to enjoy, their favorite thing about their cruise to Alaska, and so much more. We stopped for a while to learn about a reservoir that was built to provide water for our entire town once upon a time, and we debated about how much bigger the structure would have to be to do that now.

What a difference today's hike was from the last time we journeyed up that trail together. A few years ago, they were quiet and winded the whole way, but this trip highlighted the way they've developed both physically and in their interpersonal skills. I could certainly tell that my sister and brother-in-law have been strategically engaging their boys in conversations.

After they left that night, I considered the gift of being present. I thought about how grateful I was for that time with them and how amazing it was to learn so much about them—and to make new discoveries together in such a short time. These two young boys were excellent company!

LET'S TALK

Leslie

Conversations have always been central to our family's dynamic. David and I prioritize special dates with our kids, allowing us to connect and learn about their interests. These shared experiences provide valuable conversation starters. Because we experience so much life together, we always have interesting things to think about!

Sometimes talking with your preteen can be a struggle. As we noted in chapter 1, there's both a lot of little kid in them and also more maturity than we may realize. Sometimes, a preteen may struggle with which side of them will be on display. They may even go back and forth within the same conversation! No matter how difficult it may be to start a conversation, making the effort is worth it.

You may be reading this and be thinking, "Wow, you make conversations sound so easy." There are moments when we set aside the time and try to be intentional and interested, and our preteens still don't want to talk. If preteens feel that you're coming to them with any ulterior motive, they will shut down.

Exchange Insights

Kids this age deal with a lot of insecurity. So look them in the eyes as you talk to them, showing them the respect you would give another adult in a conversation. Be bold enough to engage with them at a heart level. There's room for silly conversations. In fact, most of the time you spend talking with your preteen may be silly. Still, look for the moments when you spot a tender moment or the softening of a heart. It's a signal that the door is open for you to go a little deeper. You may be amazed at what you find!

Their fresh perspectives, unjaded by years of life experience, can offer insightful wisdom.

Rather than simply imparting wisdom, ask open-ended questions like, "What do you think about that?" or "What did you hear about that?" and "What do you think the Bible says about that?" Give them space to share their thoughts. They often have more insight than they realize. Sometimes, they preach to themselves, and we don't need to be the ones always saying, "Do this" or "Don't do that." When they arrive at truth through their own reflection, it makes a profound difference in their lives.

I was humbled time and time again when I talked to my kids and they opened their hearts to me. At this stage they can think some deep thoughts, and I found they can even teach their parents some lessons. Their fresh perspectives, unjaded by years of life experience, can offer insightful wisdom. A mutual exchange of ideas will deepen your relationship and broaden your own understanding. Embrace the humility of being taught by your child, and express gratitude for these enlightening moments.

When Conversation Includes Correction

Sometimes we need to address a situation that requires clarification or correction. Use questions wisely to understand the circumstances. This will go a long way in getting the information you need. Keep in mind that questions prick the conscience, whereas accusations harden the will. If you go into a conversation ready to lower the boom, you'll often find that you'll shut down any opportunity for teaching or discipleship.

Speaking firmly or harshly and demanding an answer will build a wall around your child's heart. And that is counterproductive to what we're trying to achieve!

On the other hand, when you approach the conversation with a calm, non-accusatory tone and ask questions like, "Why did you think that was a good idea?" or "What made you say yes to that?," you create space to understand what's really going on. Maintain gentle eye contact and an open posture to show you're genuinely interested in their thought process. Offer a knowing smile to show you understand the impulsiveness of this stage.

Asking questions of our preteens is also a great way to allay our own fears. We've all jumped to the worst possible conclusion after seeing our child's actions. But by asking questions, I often learned that their path wasn't rooted in malice, but rather immaturity or poor decision-making. These questions served as an opportunity to discuss the importance of wise choices in a practical, relatable way. This is an ideal time to illustrate the concept of cause and effect, showing how actions inevitably lead to consequences.

When Your Preteen Acts Out

We never knew where we'd find them, but our daughter left little notes of encouragement and love for us on our bed, beside the coffee maker, or stuck inside our Bibles, so we'd find them early the next morning. She couldn't have known how often her little notes were the exact balm my soul needed. This is one I recently found:

"Dear Mama, You are by far the best mother anyone could ever ask for. I love you so much! You are so loving and encouraging to all of us. I have no idea how you manage to still be so amazing and cool while taking care of all our needs and TTD [our ministry Teach Them Diligently]. *I love you so extreamly* [her spelling] *much. XOXO"*

Since she was a little one, she'd always been precious. I couldn't find another word that adequately described her. The first girl after a couple of rough-and-tumble boys, she had been born tiny, bald, and incredibly sweet. (I'm pretty sure I saw her daddy melt into a puddle on the delivery room floor as soon as he saw her.)

But something happened to my precious girl when she became a preteen. She was still there, but somehow, so was a little bully. Her favorite victim was her younger sister, three and a half years her junior, who touched her stuff and messed up their room, much to her dismay. It was a strange time because the one who had rarely been in trouble before found herself in a constant state of feeling like she was disappointing us and acting like she was out of control.

We had a lot of hard conversations during that period of her life. Her dad and I were trying to figure out where this different personality came from (and how it had eaten up the precious one!), and we were trying to help her understand that the admonition to "be kind to one another" we talked about when she was little still applied now that she was getting older.

When asking your preteen questions about their behavior, it's not just about finding solutions—it's about getting to the heart of why they did what they did. Many times in our conversations, my children would break down crying, saying, "I don't know why I did it. I'm so bad," which grieved me deeply. But this is where they are. Their brains are changing, their hormones are rushing, and their bodies are growing in ways they don't understand. They might do things they don't want to because they feel out of control.

The "because I had the power to, so I did," mindset is really prevalent with preteens. Being aware of those developmental changes we talked about earlier helps you guide your children through these times and help them understand that just because "I can" doesn't mean "I should."

Pay attention when you see behaviors pop up that seem out of the ordinary; for extra time with you may be exactly what they're craving.

Just as when our older daughter was being mean to our younger daughter, there will be many times when you catch your child in the act, and you feel justified in coming down hard on them. But by approaching them with questions, you can understand the reasoning behind their actions. Other reasons that often factor into poor, uncharacteristic, or confusing behavior include a desire for attention, learned behavior from watching their friends or families they see on TV, or frustration and jealousy. Often, our children don't even realize that they're jockeying for attention or trying to take the spotlight off another child when they behave this way. They might not recognize this as sin. We read in Romans 7 about how even Paul struggled with doing right things and not doing wrong things.

As a parent, pay attention when you see behaviors pop up that seem out of the ordinary; for extra time with you may be exactly what they're craving, and you may find that their hearts are open and ready for some great conversations while you're hanging out.

Delving into unusual behaviors—even unkindness or worse among siblings—and trying to discover where these are coming from will take effort, and you might not resolve issues instantly. Take the time to engage in conversations with them about their actions and also about God's perfect plan in putting together your family. The lessons they learn in their youth will be foundational as they start to build their own families when they're grown.

The Beauty of a Lasting Connection

Not too long ago, as my daughter Lizzie Gray and I sat side by side at the day spa, surrounded by the soothing hum of conversation and the aroma of scented lotions, she shared stories of her recent weekend with friends. I listened intently, taking in every word as she described their astonishment at the openness of her relationship with me, her dad, and her siblings. These friends, with their own varied upbringings, couldn't fathom the dynamic Lizzie Gray described. A warmth spread through me as I realized the fruit of years of intentional parenting and prayer. David and I hadn't been perfect, but we'd strived to build a home rooted in biblical principles, saturated with love.

"My friends kept asking how we could talk about things so freely," Lizzie Gray said, shaking her head in amusement. "They just couldn't get over how different our family is." In this moment, as my now-married daughter freely shared her life with me, I knew those efforts had cultivated a bond that would endure through the seasons of life.

The road to open communication wasn't always easy, but it is worth it. Our home was filled with six unique, imperfect people, each navigating their own growth phases. God has forged our lives and hearts together through shared beliefs, experiences, and through the gift of conversations. Our bond was made up of one talk after another—some silly and others serious. Yet abundant laughter and love is the result, not only through the challenging adolescent years, but for all the years to come.

TELLING STORIES
Tricia

One of my kids' favorite things is to hear stories. They like stories about when John and I, or their grandparents, were growing up. These tales of antics, mishaps, and adventures from a bygone era offer a glimpse into our past. (Although even using the word bygone makes me feel old!) Through these shared stories, our family history comes alive, and our children see that they are part of something bigger than themselves.

Hard Stories

Most of us have stories from the past that are difficult to tell. They may be about hard things done to us, or mistakes we made. For many years I trembled at just the idea of telling my kids about my teen years. Seeking love in all the wrong places, I became sexually active at a young age. The first time I found myself pregnant was at age fifteen. When I went to a clinic for advice, they made me believe that a simple procedure, or in their words "scraping a few cells away," could make this problem disappear. What teen doesn't want what they think is an easy way out of their mistake? Yet as soon as I left that clinic, I regretted my decision. And when I became pregnant again by the same boyfriend a few years later, I made a different choice.

For years, I carried the heavy burden of my sins until I realized that Jesus had washed *all* my sins away the moment I surrendered my life to Him. And while I found healing through my deepening relationship with Jesus—and in the community of other women—I still worried about having to tell my kids.

Yet as my three oldest kids neared their preteen years, God called me to share my testimony in my church. My desire was to share my heartbreak and God's healing. I wanted to offer hope to other women who carried heavy burdens. Knowing I wanted my children to first hear my story from me, and not from someone else who'd heard me at church, I told them about my past and my pain. Their tears, hugs, and unconditional love was a healing balm.

Then, as the years passed, I discovered that it gave them a voice on the matter. More than once I heard from a youth leader or adult friend about how one of my children related my story with other teens their age, sharing how what seems like an easy answer can bring decades of pain.

Although it's difficult, revealing our past mistakes with authenticity and humility can help our children learn the consequences of wrong living without having to face those consequences themselves. When I share my story, I also tell them that all of us make mistakes, and no matter what they've done they can turn to God—and to me and John—and we will always be there to love them. It's a truth they can believe because they see us as living, walking examples of that.

Parables

A parable is a simple story used to illustrate a moral or spiritual lesson. Jesus told parables in the Gospels to share complex ideas through the use of story. Storytelling can impart wisdom to our child in a way that has them engaged, yet they don't feel as if you're lecturing. I clearly remember the rapt attention on my children's faces when, right in the middle of one homeschool day, I told them I had a story to tell them.

"I have a friend who moved to the city with her three little kids," I began. "She moved to a part of town where there were many bad influences, so she built a tall fence around her yard to keep her kids safe while they were playing outside unsupervised. The kids promised to stay inside the fence, but soon, people outside started taunting them, daring them to climb over for a thrill. The outsiders wanted to exploit these children—even hurt them—but the kids didn't know that. More than once my friend reminded her kids of the dangers. She told them to make good choices and respect the fence.

"At first, my friend's children obeyed, but the temptations became too great, and they stepped closer and closer to the fence. Curious about what they were missing out on, they even climbed on the fence to peek over, which is exactly what the people on the other side wanted."

As I continued with my story, describing how the temptation persisted and sharing the potential risks of climbing the fence, my children began to shift uncomfortably.

"Someone needs to stop those kids! They could fall over, or someone could grab them and they'll get hurt!" one of my preteens called out.

"Yes, my friend put up the fence to protect them, but she can't watch her kids day and night." Then I took a deep breath. "That's kind of like the internet, isn't it?" I asked gently. "We trust you to make good choices, but there are dangers lurking online. People with bad intentions try to tempt you to do things that could put you at risk. Just like the fence, having rules about internet use is a way to keep you safe while still allowing freedom."

The lights went on then. My preteens saw the parallel and understood the reasoning behind the boundaries we'd set. Through this simple story, my children were able to grasp the importance of digital boundaries without feeling lectured or targeted. Of course that's not to say they never neared the fence or tried to peek over. They did! And we'd again remind them of the dangers—relating again the story about the fence.

This is the power of storytelling in parenting. By illustrating principles through relatable narratives, we can help our children understand and internalize important values in a subtle, non-confrontational way. Stories have a way of sticking with us, making them a potent tool for imparting wisdom that will guide our kids well into the future.

UNCONDITIONAL LOVE

Tricia

Adopting preteens brought a unique set of challenges. Our new children came with a lifetime of experiences already under their belts, and understandably, they eyed us with uncertainty. John and I found ourselves navigating uncharted waters, questioning what to discuss openly and what to address later. When our preteens did open up, their questions often felt like tests, probing our sincerity. They would ask things like, "Would you visit me if I went to jail?" Or "If I married someone of the same sex would you come to my wedding?" Questions like these at first brought a lot of fears and worries, until I realized what they were: *tests.*

Wounded by past disappointments, our newly adopted preteens struggled to accept the concept of unconditional love and the promise of permanent commitment. Also, when it came to questions like these, John came up with the best answer (guided by God, no doubt!). He'd say, "If we ever have a situation like that, we'll seek God and allow Him to guide us in the right thing to do. But know that I love you unconditionally. I'll always want to make sure you know that—now and in the future."

Yet showing unconditional love is crucial. When I volunteered at a pregnancy care center, we were taught to control our reactions. When kids come to you with something shocking, control your jaw drop.

You might not know how to respond immediately, so it's okay to say, "Give me five minutes, I need to check something," and then come back. This gives you time to breathe and prepare. Show them that you love them unconditionally. We all mess up and struggle, but we are here for each other. Let them know they are loved no matter what.

Also, at this stage kids often still want loving physical touch like hugs, even though it makes them feel awkward. Often I'd ask my preteens, "Do you want a hug?" There have been times they told me no, but the majority of times they've said yes, and they opened their arms for a big embrace.

One thing I recently learned is to let the child be the first to release the hug. Surprisingly there are times they just want to cling on, and that's okay.

As we reflect on our journey of adopting and raising preteens, we're reminded that family is about more than blood ties; it's about the unbreakable bonds formed through love, commitment, shared experiences, and lots of conversations. I mean *lots*! We have shared stories, experiences, beliefs, and regrets, and we've listened to heartache and hopes—and a lot of nonsense, if truth be told. But I know now that every conversation was another link in a chain binding us together.

Taking time for these conversations hasn't always been easy, but with each passing day, we've seen that the time was well spent. Our adopted preteens are now adults between the ages of nineteen and twenty-four. And while there are still challenges, the core principles remain the same—open communication, unconditional love, and a rock-solid faith. This was true for our biological children too!

Conversations aren't always easy, but they are something our kids can carry into adulthood with them even after so many trinkets or hobbies from their childhood are left behind. None of us can guide our children daily through their lives, but our shared stories and conversations can.

*   *   *

This is our prayer for families in this season—that the preteen years may be navigated with joy, and that the assurance of a timelessly enduring relationship, built on God's principles, may be the legacy passed down to the next generation. The connections fostered now will remain a blessing long after the children have grown and begun lives of their own.

Chapter Eight

ACTIVE LISTENING

*Listen First to Spark Meaningful Conversations
with Your Preteen*

A ctive listening is one of the most vital skills we can develop as parents, especially for our preteen kids. Sometimes this means dedicating a significant chunk of time to subjects that don't particularly interest us, like a detailed discussion on Mario Kart strategies or the nuances of their latest cartoon drawing. But here's the thing—those forty minutes of listening to their passions often pave the way for the last ten minutes, where they finally share what's really on their hearts.

HEART-TO-HEART TALKS

Tricia

With a large family, carving out individual time can be a challenge. We have ten kids, and though only four are still at home, finding one-on-one moments remains tricky. So I've learned to get creative. When I'm running errands, I'll take one child along. These trips can last a couple of hours, and it's usually in the last stretch, just before we head home, that meaningful conversations happen. That's when they open up about their worries and concerns.

Late nights are another prime time for heart-to-heart talks. My husband excels at this more than I do. Around ten or eleven o'clock, when the day is winding down and everything is quiet, our kids start asking those deep, sometimes theological questions—like about Adam and Eve's life after the fall or how all of the animals fit on Noah's ark. It's in these slowed-down moments, when the hustle of the day has faded, that their thoughts and questions surface.

Yes, sometimes we're absolutely exhausted. There are nights when I only want to close my eyes and drift off. But I try to stay awake (or John does!), even if it's just for another thirty minutes, to keep the conversation going. Those moments of active listening, even when we're tired, are invaluable. They show our kids that we're there for them, truly present, and ready to listen to whatever is on their minds and hearts.

LISTEN MORE THAN TALK
Tricia

In a world filled with distractions, giving someone our undivided attention is a rare and powerful gift. In response to my question about "active listening" with preteens on Facebook, my friend Christin shared a valuable insight: "When my kids wanted to talk to me about a problem, I asked myself, *Am I listening to support or listening to solve?* This helped me understand the true nature of our conversation and respond appropriately. Sometimes they just needed to vent and know I was there to love them as they handled the situation. Other times they wanted advice on how to navigate the situation."

My friend Karen, who is a mom of two preteens and a teacher of preteens, put it this way: "Active listening means hearing what your child is really asking. Often, their words don't match what is happening in their bodies, brains, or spirits. Rephrasing their words back to them is crucial: 'So what I'm hearing from you is that. . . .' Active listening also implies listening without an answer at the ready, without judgment or other motivation. Sometimes, the simple act of talking through a challenge allows children to come to an answer or decision on their own. Other times, they'll need our guidance and input, but we cannot guide them effectively if we don't understand what is happening underneath the surface."

My friend Ann reminded me that our role when we talk to our preteens isn't to act like a friend. "When they talk with you, they generally want a parent's perspective. Otherwise, they'd be talking to their friends. Listen as a parent, not a friend, although you can be a friendly (or not) parent."

Of course, this doesn't mean when we sit down with our preteen they'll immediately share what's going on. As I mentioned before, time away matters. Most preteens still enjoy spending time with their parents, so they'll likely be enthusiastic or at least willing to join you if invited on a special outing. These casual, side-by-side interactions can foster some of the best conversations you'll have during this phase. Talk flows naturally, allowing you to share your thoughts and truly hear what's on their mind. These moments are invaluable for maintaining open and honest communication as they age.

Don't miss these opportunities. Instead of fearing the future, embrace these chances to connect. Simply be present, talk about everyday things, and show interest in what's important to them. This is how you lay the foundation for a strong, communicative relationship during the preteen years and beyond.[12]

Listen Now to Be Trusted to Listen Later

You'll have conversations with your kids that might not interest you inherently, but by engaging in these seemingly insignificant conversations, you show them that what matters to them matters to you. My friend Traci told me, "I call it the ministry of presence. Sitting with my teen, playing her style of music, waiting for her to talk will offer the richest conversations. Absolutely worth it."

"Why should our kids care about what we have to say if we can't spare a moment to really soak in that new crazy thing they are excited about?" my friend Kristen pointed out. "Respect goes both ways. If you want respect from your kiddo for your beliefs and ideals, show respect and attention when they share theirs with you. Even when their favorite topics are different than yours. *Especially* when they are different."

This habit of listening builds a foundation that can be built on. As kids age and face high school or adulthood challenges, they'll know they can still come to you. Deep conversations in the teen years are grown from many moments of listening to the little things. Because at this stage of life, the things we consider "little things" are actually big deals for preteens. By sticking with them and engaging, you unlock insights into their hearts. Our kids know we're available, and coming to us feels natural, which is what we want.

Believe Them

At least a few times a week, one of my children will come to me and say, "Mom, can I talk to you alone?" It's times like these that I stop what I'm doing because I know that the conversation is going to be one that I need to focus my full attention on.

Sometimes these conversations deal with ways they've been mistreated, often by a sibling or a friend's words or actions. But there have been times when one of my kids has told me about more serious things—inappropriate things—that have been said or texted to them. Things have been said at church camp, videos have been forwarded by people they believed to be friends, and there have been times when other family members outside our home have crossed the line.

The first thing we always tell our kids is we believe them, and we will do whatever we can to make sure they feel safe, both physically and emotionally. When we are safe places for our kids, they will better be able to distinguish what is safe and unsafe. We want them to know we will believe them, and they can come to us. This is important because both John and I have had situations in the past where we weren't believed. That's a scary place for a child to be.

When John was little, he went to stay with one set of grandparents. One of his grandfathers was emotionally abusive to him. John wanted to tell his mother, but he felt certain that his mother would believe her own father over him. So John faced that abuse for weeks. Only later, when the truth came out, did John's mom understand everything that was happening. She also told John she'd always believe him, especially since her father had said cruel things to her too, when she was little.

As a parent, sometimes it's hard to know how to handle situations with family members or close friends. Recently, our daughters were out of town and ended up in a situation where they didn't feel comfortable. As I listened to my daughters recounting over the phone their experiences and telling me they didn't want to be in that place anymore, I didn't hesitate. I immediately connected with a friend who lives in that area. I asked if she could pick up my girls and keep them overnight until we could get them. She immediately agreed to help. I am so thankful for a caring friend willing to help immediately!

Of course, these actions led to criticism and claims that I was making my children entitled by stepping in to help, giving my children an unrealistic sense of self-importance. This isn't true. They *are* important. It *is* important that my children feel safe. It is vital that my children know that John and I will listen to them and believe them.

The more we create a home that is filled with mutual self-respect and honor toward each other and God, the more clearly our children will recognize disrespect and dishonor. We want our children to be aware of unhealthy people and situations and steer clear of them. We help them by being willing to listen to our preteens, to believe them, and to help them remain safe to the best of our ability. This is healthy communication.

LISTENING FOR UNDERSTANDING

Leslie

Active listening can often feel like you're conversing with a four-year-old, where their thoughts seem to ramble all over the place. A ten-year-old can be the same way. It takes time for them to get to the heart of what they're really trying to say.

For both boys and girls, there's often a lot of clutter in their minds that they need to work through before they reach their main point. Practicing active listening means being patient and letting them talk until they finally wind their way around to their actual thoughts. It means actively engaging with them and asking questions in order to understand.

Proverbs 16–18 provides wisdom about listening and understanding. These passages highlight the importance of patience, wisdom, and a calm approach to resolving conflicts and guiding others. Parents have the best conversations with their preteens when they listen more than talk. You gain valuable insight into their hearts by allowing your kids to express themselves fully. This aligns with the biblical principle of being quick to listen and slow to speak.

Take Your Time

Adding to Leslie's thoughts above, one of the best things I (Tricia) learned about parenting preteens is that most things don't have to be solved immediately. Sometimes, it's best to pray about it, discuss it with your spouse, and give it some thought until the next day. Not everything requires an immediate solution.

One valuable lesson I learned from a therapist while working with our adopted kids is that when your emotional brain is turned on, your thinking brain is turned off. If your child is emotional and you keep talking, it's not registering anyway. It just frustrates them and creates division.

When you notice your child starting to get emotional—whether it's tears, tenseness, or an overwhelmed look—take a break. You might say, "I know this is a hard thing to talk about. Let's pick it up after dinner or tomorrow." When emotions are still high, postponing the conversation lets everyone calm down. Often, your child might come to you first with an apology: "I'm sorry I said this," or "I'm sorry I did that." Giving them time to think about their actions can lead to genuine remorse and reflection.

Right Timing

Even if we have wonderful conversations, our preteens will still make mistakes. They'll say or do the wrong thing, and while we don't want to let these things slide, it's also important to have conversations with our kids in a way that gives them respect and dignity.

As has been said, if your child needs to be disciplined and you're with a group of people (including their siblings), it's best to address it privately. If you scold them in front of others, it can be mortifying for them. At an age where peer perception means a lot, public reprimand can trigger defensiveness.

They might not want to show they're embarrassed, sad, or on the verge of tears, so instead, they express anger. Sad comes out as mad, and embarrassed comes out as mad too. Addressing the issue privately helps them feel respected and more open to resolving the matter.

When I say, "Let's go talk in my room," my preteen might resist, but at least it provides a safe space where they don't feel like everyone is listening and judging them.

Being vulnerable and real with your children is also crucial. Let them know you understand their feelings by saying things like, "I understand why you feel that way," or "I felt that way before when I was your age."

For example, if your child is upset because someone said something hurtful, acknowledge their feelings: "That would make me upset too. How does it make you feel when he says that?"

Let them talk and express their emotions. Once they've communicated their feelings, you can guide them gently: "I'm sorry you felt that way, but because we believe in God, we don't say those things back." This approach allows you to disciple and teach while giving them a chance to talk first.

Heart-to-heart conversations are crucial, and sometimes preteens need a safe space to talk, like on a car ride or at a coffee shop where they aren't worried about siblings overhearing.

With my girls, if there were serious matters to discuss, I would sometimes take them away for the weekend. This gave them a break from the usual environment and the freedom to talk openly. Creating a safe space for these conversations—whether it's a special outing or just a private moment—fosters a trusting relationship and helps them feel secure in sharing their hearts.

By practicing patience, avoiding embarrassment, and having meaningful heart to heart conversations, we can build strong, trusting relationships with our children. These principles help create an environment where they feel safe, respected, and understood.

* * *

Here's a quick take on some of the points we discussed in this chapter.

1. Talk to your kids in the preteen years like the intelligent, capable people they are.

2. Listen more than you talk.

3. Ensure your preteen feels safe enough to discuss their thoughts and feelings.

4. Be honest about your own struggles, mess-ups, and the questions you have.

5. Be patient, and do not force conversations. Instead, let them happen organically.

6. Encourage your preteen to think about what they believe and ask questions.

7. Even if you don't agree with your preteen's feelings or experiences, validate them.

8. Use open-ended questions to spark deeper conversations.

9. To connect with your preteen meaningfully, be empathetic.

10. When talking to preteens, be present and pay attention.

Chapter Nine

INTENTIONAL SPIRITUAL CONVERSATIONS

Words with Eternal Impact

Talking to preteens about spiritual topics can be hard, but it's an important part of helping them grow in their faith. We can encourage preteens to ask questions and talk about how they feel and what they think. Such openness fosters deeper discussions, strengthening both faith and family bonds. Through open, honest dialogue, parents create a trustworthy space for preteens to explore their faith.

SPIRITUAL MATTERS

Leslie

Raised in a devout Christian home, my parents' early conversion significantly shaped our upbringing. They ensured that my sister and I had a Christian education and were part of a vibrant church community. I'm grateful for the way my parents' early conversion significantly shaped my and my sister's upbringing. I realize not everyone has a similar experience. In fact, you may be the adult God is using to have these conversations with your children's friends or children in your church.

What I learned from my parents is to be open about faith. As they grew in their relationship with Jesus, they brought me and my sister along for the journey. God gave parents the most powerful platform in their children's lives, and we're called to use that platform to bring our children to Jesus and to be intentional in passing on a faith that sticks. We are privileged to have a front-row seat to watch our children grow in understanding, maturity, and faith.

Sadly, a Barna study about guiding children found that for many families, the time spent engaging with their children about spiritual matters starts to diminish as their children reach the tween years.[13] As the parents start to back off from spiritual discussions with their children, the tweens generally start to change their view of church as well, often losing interest in attending church. When you add in that children have access to more information about other religions and worldviews today, it's no wonder that many are confused and left wondering what's really believable.

Allow Them to Ask Difficult Questions

We aim to help our kids build a strong foundation for a faith that is truly their own. Sometimes, this process involves grappling with tough questions. These questions might scare you or challenge your own beliefs.

Your preteens may start questioning aspects of their faith, cultural norms, or things they observe in the world around them. By engaging with them and loving them through these moments of doubt and curiosity, you can help them navigate their spiritual journey.

If you don't know the answer to their questions, be honest. Admit when you don't have all the answers, and then take the opportunity to discover the answers together. Delve into God's Word or seek out other reliable sources to find the information they need. This joint effort not only strengthens their faith but also reinforces the importance of seeking truth.

Active listening means embracing uncomfortable or scary topics and turning them into learning and growth opportunities. Engage with your preteens, support them, and guide them through their difficult questions with patience and love. You want your preteen to know that you're available when they want to talk about spiritual matters and that you're a trustworthy guide. They need to be comfortable talking to you about difficult subjects or situations without fear of judgment or rebuke for asking questions. They need to see in you a guide that is sincere and authentic much more than they need to think you have all the answers. It's really awesome to dig out those answers together sometimes.

One of our boys was preparing to head to camp one summer when he was about eleven. Although he had put his faith in Jesus a few years prior, he was struggling with guilt and with the assurance that he truly was a child of God. He came to his daddy very upset that God wasn't pleased with him, and he was scared he wasn't a Christian. David had the opportunity to talk to him that day about how he could know for sure that he was truly a Christian as he led him through the book of 1 John.

In that book, the apostle John wrote, "I write these things to you who believe in the name of the Son of God so that you may know that you have eternal life" (1 John 5:13), and thirty-seven times throughout that letter, he gives us things to talk about with our children to help them know for sure that they believe. In his letter, John explains that there is one method of salvation, which is belief in Christ. He encourages us that once

As parents, we get the incredible privilege of answering questions and giving our children reasons for why we have the hope we have in Christ.

you are saved, you are always saved and no one can change that, and he says that you can know you are saved by examining the fruit of your life. Those are just a few of the topics you can discuss with your children as they are starting to make their faith their own and need to deeply understand what they believe and what that means for their relationship with God.

After that discussion, David told our son that sometimes we get uncomfortable because God is asking us to let go of something that we don't want to let go of. He was able to tell him stories of ways God had led him in that way throughout his life, and he asked our son if there was anything he was struggling with. At that point, our son confessed exactly what God had been dealing with in him, and David had the privilege of leading him through what the Bible has to say about that issue. It was a phenomenal opportunity for David to engage with him about such important things, and it was a wonderful reminder for David as well since, in the process of counseling our son, he was also brought back to the biblical truths he needed to apply to his own life each day.

First Peter 3:15 tells us that we should always be ready to give an answer or explanation for the hope that's in us. As parents, we get the incredible privilege of answering questions and giving our children reasons for why we have the hope we have in Christ, why we believe what we believe, and why we know that God is in control—even when everything we see and feel seems to be out of our control.

Can you believe God allows us to be the ones to do that? I hope that part of our calling as parents causes you joy.

For those who are unsure about your abilities to lead your children through conversations about spiritual things, I want to give you some starting points. A great reference book you may want to keep handy is *Quick Scripture Reference for Counseling* by John G. Kruis. That book takes topics that you or your children may deal with, like anger, bitterness, fear, lust, suffering, and more, and gives you verses that apply to those topics.

The Gospel

I was honored to talk to all of our children about the good news of Jesus many times as they were growing up, and I was there to pray with three of the four of them when they accepted Jesus as their personal Savior. I stand amazed that God allowed me the privilege of explaining the gospel to them, helping them understand that Jesus, who had lived a perfect life, loved them enough to die for them, even though they were sinners (Rom. 5:8). There's great hope knowing that though the wages of their sin is death and separation from God, it doesn't have to be that way, because if they accept God's free gift of salvation, they will have eternal life through Jesus Christ (Rom. 6:23).

We're further told that "if you declare with your mouth, 'Jesus is Lord,' and believe in your heart that God raised him from the dead, you will be saved" (Rom. 10:9). Confessing with your mouth and believing in your heart that Jesus is Lord is all you have to do to accept that free gift. God made it so simple for His children, so we don't want to over-complicate it for ours.

Each Christian is given the mission of being God's witnesses in Jerusalem, Judea, Samaria, and throughout the rest of the earth (Acts 1:8). As parents on a mission, your home is your Jerusalem, and you are the greatest gospel influence on your children throughout the time they're in your home. One survey notes that 68 percent of adult evangelicals chose to follow Christ by the age of fourteen, and the influence of their parents was touted as the biggest contributing factor in their conversion.[14] You have a great opportunity to impact your children for eternity through the strategic, gospel-filled conversations you have within your home.

SAFE EXPLORATION

Tricia

As parents, we have a unique opportunity to lead our children to faith in Jesus. Just as Jesus was attentive to seeking hearts, we can create an environment where our kids feel safe to explore spirituality. We've found the following steps to be a helpful framework for guiding our children toward a personal relationship with Jesus. These principles are adapted from *I Once Was Lost: What Postmodern Skeptics Taught Us About Their Path to Jesus* by Don Everts and Doug Schaupp.[15]

1. Model trustworthy Christianity. Live out your faith authentically, demonstrating love, grace, and joy.

2. Spark curiosity about Jesus. Share engaging stories from the Bible and discuss how faith impacts daily life.

3. Encourage them to ask questions. Create a safe space where your child feels comfortable asking about God and spirituality.

4. Inspire them to consider making changes in their own lives. As your child matures, talk about the importance of aligning actions and beliefs.

5. Invite them to have a personal relationship with Jesus. When the time is right, clearly explain the gospel and invite them to make a personal commitment to follow Jesus.

This model isn't a formula but a flexible guide. Pray for your child and trust the Holy Spirit to work in their heart. Like Jesus, be patient and focus on those teachable moments when your child is receptive. Invest in these conversations, and you may enjoy seeing your child surrender their life to Jesus. When it comes to leading our children to Christ, we never know when it will happen, but for many of our children, it happens during the preteen years.

The funny thing is, because of homeschooling, I did most of the planting. I spent the most time on Bible lessons, reading, and devotional books. Yet it was John who did most of the harvesting. A conversation would come up on a walk or doing yardwork, and John would pull up a porch chair and take the time to talk.

During one season, one of our preteens accepted Christ this way, and then she told her sister, who did the same the next night, and they both talked to their brother. Each urged the other to "take time to talk to Dad so you can give your heart to Jesus too." I'm thankful that John and I could work together as a team—with the Holy Spirit, of course.

THE POWER OF WALKING THE TALK
Tricia

Have you ever heard the phrase, "Your walk talks more than your talk talks"? This simple yet profound saying captures a fundamental truth about parenting: our actions often speak louder than words. As Christian parents, how we live out our faith can have a far greater impact on our children than anything we say.

Imagine your daily actions are like a sermon your children are constantly hearing. Every choice you make, every word you speak, and every action you take communicates volumes about your values and beliefs. When it comes to nurturing their faith, your children are more likely to be influenced by what they see you do than by what they hear you say.

One of the most powerful ways to teach your children about faith is to let them see you living it out. When they observe you reading your Bible, they learn that God's Word is important and worth studying. When they see you praying, they understand that communication with God is a vital part of everyday life. And when they witness you seeking God's guidance in decisions, big and small, they grasp that faith is not just for Sundays but for every moment of every day.

Authenticity in your faith journey is crucial. Children are incredibly perceptive and can easily spot when someone is being insincere. Show them that your faith is not just a set of rules to follow but a relationship with a loving God. Share your struggles and victories with them. Let them know that it's okay to have questions and doubts, and that faith is a journey as well as a destination.

For instance, involve your children in the process when you face a challenging situation. Let them see you turning to prayer and Scripture for comfort and guidance. Explain how you are trusting God to provide or to give you wisdom. These real-life examples will stick with them far longer than a lecture on faith ever could.

Consistency in your walk of faith is essential. It's not about being perfect but about being consistent. Your children will learn that faith is a constant, guiding presence in your life, not something that is only relevant in certain situations or on specific days.

When your children see you prioritizing church attendance, serving others, and living out Christian principles, they will understand that your faith is the foundation of your life. These consistent actions reinforce the importance of living a life that honors God.

Your interactions with others also serve as a powerful testimony to your children. How you treat people, especially in difficult situations, speaks volumes about the love and grace of Christ. When you show kindness, forgiveness, and patience, your children learn about the character of God. They see the gospel in action.

It's also important to demonstrate how to handle failures and mistakes. Admitting when you're wrong and seeking forgiveness, both from God and from those you've wronged, teaches your children about repentance and the power of grace. It shows them that it's okay to be imperfect and that God's love covers all.

* * *

Ultimately, the goal is to inspire your children to pursue their own authentic faith journey. By consistently living out your faith in front of them, you provide a road map they can follow. Encourage them to read their Bibles, pray, and seek God's guidance. Celebrate their spiritual milestones and be there to support them through their questions and struggles.

Remember, your walk talks more than your talk talks. Let your life be a living testimony of God's love and faithfulness. As your children watch and learn from you, they will be equipped to develop a faith that is strong, genuine, and deeply personal.

Chapter Ten

SERVE WITH HEART

Why Showing God's Love Through Service Matters

Serving others is a crucial aspect of the faith journey because it teaches preteens to care about others and develop compassion. When preteens engage in acts of service, they learn to look beyond themselves and see the needs of those around them. This shift in perspective fosters empathy and a deeper understanding of the importance of helping others.

ACTING IN LOVE

Tricia

A few years ago my three youngest children and I visited the doctor in a questionable part of town. (This doctor believes in caring for under-resourced kids, which I love!) We were in a small strip mall, and I'd just loaded up all the kids into the car when my daughter Alyssa noticed a man in a wheelchair approaching us. He was an older man with only one leg. He was thin, but he had kind eyes. He motioned to me, and instead of starting my engine, I rolled down the window.

"Ma'am, do you happen to have a few dollars for food? I'm so hungry."

Personally, I don't believe in giving out money. I've seen what it's used for by those whose addictions have a hold of them, but I will—when it is possible—help with food.

"Sir, I don't have cash to give you, but I have some food here." And I did! It "just so happened" that after Bible study that morning, my leader gave me a sack lunch because she knew I couldn't stay for fellowship. I handed over the sandwich and cinnamon rolls.

I also had donuts. You see, it also "just so happened" that I'd found a Mexican bakery that morning and had bought some special treats for my grandma. After handing over the lunch, I pulled the largest donut from the box and handed that over too.

"Ma'am?" the man asked, his eyes bright. "Is this cream-filled?"

"I'm not sure, sir."

It turns out it was! As I drove away, I realized I hadn't been thinking about modeling service and caring for others for my kids, but that's exactly what had happened, and on the way home, we had a long conversation about how we could serve others in similar situations as that man.

IT'S OKAY TO "DRAG YOUR KIDS ALONG"

Tricia

As a mom, there are many things that I want to teach my kids that are important. I want my kids to know how to cook and how to clean. I want them to be well-educated and respectful. I want them to love God and others, but I don't simply want love to be by words alone but by deeds.

Service doesn't mean you help everyone. It instead means there is one person God will bring into your path.

With my three older children, there were days I felt very guilty because I "dragged them along" as I served at our local pregnancy care center. They also helped me watch the kids of teen moms. They folded baby clothes. And they served in children's church.

Looking back now, teaching my kids to serve (which was what I was doing) has turned out to be one of the greatest benefits of their lives. Cory serves his wife and children and cares for his in-laws with health challenges. Leslie Joy is serving as a missionary in Europe. Nathan spends much time pouring into his younger siblings, taking them to events and having game and movie nights. Service isn't something they do to earn brownie points, but something that took root deep within them. How? By seeing me reaching out to the person God has put before me, offering what I have, and urging them to do the same.

Service doesn't mean you help everyone. It instead means there is someone God will bring into your path. You show the love of Jesus when you see that person not as a bother but as someone who needs a glimpse of Jesus' love that day. What could be greater than teaching our children that?

Put Action with Your Faith

Reading God's Word and praying are essential, but it's equally important to put your faith into action by serving others as we read in James 2:17. One of the best ways to help kids stay connected to church as adults is to get them involved in church activities and service opportunities. Volunteering together as a family can make a lasting impact.

When my kids were little, they helped me at my booth during homeschool conferences. (They still do!) We went on mission trips together. For example, when Nathan was twelve, we traveled to the Czech Republic for our first mission trip. These experiences not only strengthened their faith but also taught them the importance of serving others.

Getting your kids involved in church and service activities will help them walk out their faith meaningfully. By actively participating in these activities, they learn the value of community, compassion, and commitment to their faith, which can guide them throughout their lives.

SERVING WITH YOUR PRETEEN

Leslie

A memory popped up on my Facebook feed a month or so ago. It showed my daughters and me with smiles and our sleeves rolled up. We were wearing the same teal T-shirts that the rest of our church family were wearing that afternoon as we served our community through a Family Fun Fest we were hosting. Our eyes looked a little tired because the night before we had finished a long weekend of serving homeschool families in Georgia through Teach Them Diligently, and we had driven home late Saturday night to make sure we could be there for the outreach on Sunday afternoon.

Natural Blueprint for Serving

Like so many other things in our lives, the way our children served alongside us was not as much a premeditated, strategic plan as it was the way God led us as we sought His face every day for how we should live our lives and raise our children. I believe that's the most misunderstood part about biblical parenting. It's not based on a long checklist. It's based on a relationship with God, who sees your family and knows His plans for you. The teach-them-diligently passage in Deuteronomy that our ministry is named after gives parents a natural blueprint for passing on a faith that sticks to their children. You simply engage with them in all areas of your life naturally.

As you walk, as you do dishes, as you drive them places, as you eat your meals—as you do just about anything—you can find ways to weave faith and life lessons into your conversations. Serving together is a great way to not only talk to them about a faith that sticks but also to allow them to see the impact their life of faith can make on the lives of others.

Including our children in everything God allowed us to do was normal to our family routine. David and I learned early on that you teach what you know, but you reproduce who you are. Understanding that we reproduce who we are drove us to endeavor to be the types of believers, parents, spouses, and people that we would want to see our children become as they grew up. We've spent much time studying how God's Word tells us to live and trying to model that for our children. Showing compassion to others and making a difference in their lives through service, offering an empathetic listening ear, meeting their needs, and more are concepts that we see in Scripture and that we see modeled by Jesus Himself during His time on earth.

The Transformative Power of Serving Others

Helping others can profoundly change a person's faith and give them a stronger sense of purpose. Even small acts of kindness can have a significant impact, and involving preteens in service projects can help them develop a lifelong heart for service.

Family service projects can be both fun and meaningful, providing opportunities for everyone to grow in their faith while making a difference in people's lives. Working together on service projects strengthens family bonds and creates lasting memories. Whether volunteering at a local food bank, participating in a community clean-up, or organizing a charity event, these shared experiences instill values of generosity and teamwork.

Through outreach activities, families can share their faith and extend their impact beyond their immediate community. Engaging in service projects allows families to demonstrate their beliefs in action, providing a tangible expression of their faith. These efforts can inspire others and create opportunities for meaningful conversations about faith and compassion.

Don't forget small acts of kindness. They also can have a big impact. Encouraging preteens to participate in service projects, no matter how small, helps them develop a heart for service that will last their whole lives. Simple gestures, like helping a neighbor with groceries or writing thank-you notes to community workers, teach preteens that even the smallest acts of kindness can make a difference.

As we have all served together in various ways through the years, we've seen our children grow in their ability to communicate with people from all backgrounds and walks of life, for they've been able to get beyond the fear of awkward interactions to see those in need as being made in the image of God just like they are. One Sunday evening after church, David and I went to dinner with our pastor and his wife. Our children had a pizza dinner with the teens at church, and our oldest, who had his driver's license, planned to drive them all home afterward. During dinner, I got a phone call from Camden, telling us they had gotten a flat tire on the way home from church, and there was no jack in the car. They were stranded near an alley downtown.

David and I quickly paid for our food and headed to help them. When we got to where they were, we saw the kids, who were 16, 14, 13, and 10 at the time, talking to a homeless man beside the car. They had brought some leftover pizza from the fellowship with them, and they were sharing it with the gentleman, along with a gospel presentation about how much Jesus loved him. I admit I was fearful when I drove up and saw them talking to him. He was rough-looking, and I quickly rushed to their side.

"Your kids looked me in the eye, ma'am. Most people don't do that," he noted. That gentleman heard about Jesus that day.

As David and Camden fixed the tire, though, that gentleman stood there talking to me. "They looked me in the eye, ma'am. Most people don't do that," he noted, and I marveled at the impact God had allowed them to make on him just by treating him like a real human being instead of a pariah. The girls and I continued to talk to him about life and faith until the tire was fixed. That gentleman heard about Jesus that day, and this mama learned a big lesson about trusting God with my children—even in dark alleyways downtown. I had always prayed that God would use them to impact the world for the sake of His name, and that night, He certainly used them to impact one man without a home in this world for the sake of His name.

Serving together has also taught them the value of teamwork and strengthened the bonds we have as a family. Our biggest service project together has been through Teach Them Diligently. Our children have been involved since the very beginning of this ministry, initially making up the "junior team," and then learning how to do many tasks involved in producing the events and resources we offer all along the way.

They've seen firsthand the effect that one person not doing their job has on the rest of our ability to reach people, so they've learned that they're needed. They've understood the importance of each team member in accomplishing our mission, and they have gained a sense of ownership over the mission. Their continued involvement now as adults is one of the things David and I are most grateful for. Serving together in that way through the years has given us opportunities to pray together, travel together, and share stories of God's provision and grace together. God has used those shared experiences of serving others together to knit our family together tightly.

Getting Preteens Involved in Service Projects

Getting preteens involved in service projects is a powerful way to help them learn to care about others and find a sense of purpose in life. At this stage, children are beginning to form their own identities and understand their place in the world.

Encourage them to choose projects that interest them, whether it's helping at a local animal shelter, participating in community clean-ups, or supporting food drives. These experiences can ignite a passion for helping others and foster a lifelong commitment to service.

There are countless ways families can serve together, both locally and beyond. Here are a few ideas and examples to get started:

VOLUNTEER AT LOCAL ORGANIZATIONS: Contact local non-profits, shelters, or food banks to see how your family can help. Many organizations welcome family groups to assist with sorting donations, serving meals, or providing companionship to residents.

NEIGHBORHOOD ACTS OF KINDNESS: Simple acts, like mowing a neighbor's lawn, shoveling snow, or delivering baked goods can brighten someone's day and foster a sense of community. Encourage your preteens to identify needs in your neighborhood and devise creative ways to address them.

ADOPT A HIGHWAY OR PARK: Participate in a local program to clean and maintain a section of a highway or a park. This not only helps the environment but also instills a sense of pride and ownership in your community.

HOST A FUNDRAISER: Organize a bake sale, car wash, or charity run to raise funds for a cause your family cares about. Involve your preteens in planning and executing the event to teach them organizational and leadership skills.

INTERNATIONAL MISSION TRIPS: For those looking to make a global impact, consider joining or organizing mission trips. These trips provide invaluable cultural experiences and allow your family to serve those in need around the world.

Teaching preteens to have a heart for service is essential in helping them become kind, caring individuals who contribute positively to the world. Encourage them to look beyond their needs and recognize the importance of helping others. Discuss the impact of their actions and celebrate their efforts, no matter how small. Share stories of kindness and service from your own life or from others and emphasize the positive changes these acts bring to individuals and communities.

Service as a Career

An unexpected outcome of serving together was how our family service affected my children's career choices. Working with children through our events led my older son to serve at a ministry in Indianapolis that served under-resourced communities while pursuing a degree in the Bible. Now, he's working for a business for a missions organization, recruiting teachers to serve in preschool ministries abroad.

My younger son teaches middle schoolers in a local inner-city charter school, and my older daughter is the event coordinator for Teach Them Diligently. The skills they learned along the way and the type of service they could do growing up had a tangible impact on the paths they took once they graduated from high school and started their adult lives. Encouraging your children to serve alongside you will give them valuable life skills such as organization, problem-solving, and time management and can expose them to career opportunities they may have never considered before.

Serving Others as an Expression of Faith

Serving others is a fundamental aspect of our faith journey. Jesus modeled a life of service, and by following His example, we grow closer to God and deepen our faith. Acts of service reflect God's love and grace, reinforcing the principles we learn through Scripture. By serving others, we not only help those in need but also strengthen our own spiritual lives.

Serving as a family can be a powerful way to grow closer. It creates shared experiences that bond family members together, fosters open communication, and builds a supportive environment where everyone feels valued. These shared acts of service remind us of our collective responsibility to care for others and to live out our faith in tangible ways.

* * *

Integrating service into your family life not only strengthens your faith but also shapes your preteens into compassionate, caring individuals. By getting involved in service projects, working together as a family, and leading by example, you create a legacy of kindness and generosity that will impact your children and their world.

Chapter Eleven

BRANCH OUT

Help Your Preteen Build Strong Relationships

As parents, we can help our preteens be bold about building relationships. Encouraging preteens to participate in activities or join a group—even if it's a stretch for them—can help them build confidence and form new friendships. Allowing preteens to interact with people of all ages helps them build communication skills, which will prove invaluable as they continue to grow and mature.

A WEEK TO REMEMBER

Leslie

I worked at a Christian camp in North Carolina for four summers when I was in high school and college, and I was able to get to know a whole lot of girls through serving as a waitress and then as a counselor there.

One of my campers stands out more than all the rest, and God has used her to influence my life in many ways, even though I haven't seen her since the summer of 1992. "Tina" came from a horrible background, and she was as hard and broken as you'd imagine she'd be, coming from a home reeking of all kinds of abuse. She was difficult to be around, and her attitude and actions throughout the week of camp made it seem like she wanted to ruin the week for me and the other six girls in our cabin.

She griped about everything, and she wasn't willing to try anything. She was like an anchor that held us all back from having fun or even having good conversations. By Thursday afternoon, I was done with her. No more catering to her whining and complaining. I was determined that I wasn't going to allow her to ruin the remaining two days our group had together, so I told the girls that, as a cabin, we were going to go to the obstacle course on the other side of the creek to try the challenges there.

To get to Venture Valley, you had to walk across a rope bridge that spanned the creek. I sent all the girls happily across, but when it was Tina's turn, she froze in fear. To this day, I'm not sure what came over me, but I stepped in behind her and told her there was nowhere for her to go but over. I assured her I would go with her, but she had to take the steps.

The guttural screams she let out the entire time she was on the bridge would have made you think she was being beaten or that she had just lost the most precious thing in her life, but after what seemed like hours, she made it across the short bridge to the cheers of the other girls. (I was so proud of their attitudes.)

Tina seemed to enjoy Venture Valley more than anything we had tried to do. At dinner, she actually smiled for the first time that week, and I marveled at the difference that made in how she looked. After I turned off the lights that night, I heard her voice from the bunk below mine: "Good night, Leslie. I love you." With tears rolling down my face, I told her I loved her too, and I wondered how many times in her short, tragic life she'd felt like telling someone she loved them. And I wondered if anyone ever said it to her.

She was totally different on Friday: joyful, open, and happy to be included in things with the rest of the cabin. I had the opportunity to share with her the love of Jesus that surpasses anything she could ever know here on earth, and she was eager to know more.

Tina had never had anyone believe in her enough to push her, or care enough about her to take an interest in her. As a result, she pushed everyone away and put up walls that made reaching her heart virtually impossible. But then she had nowhere left to go but forward, and she did so with the assurance that I would stick right beside her—and something changed.

DO HARD THINGS

Leslie

As parents, we have the opportunity to show our children that kind of support and to encourage them that we believe they can do hard things. Preteens tend to shy away from things that make them feel insecure out of fear that they'll fail or look foolish in front of others. At this stage of their lives, their self-worth is often tied to their achievements as they undergo so many changes. They also care a lot more about what others think of them, often making them retreat into hiding to avoid being thought poorly of. We parents can recognize and bolster their confidence.

As you encourage preteens to step out of their comfort zones, be sure you're keeping an open line of communication so you can help them work through any hurts or misunderstandings they may experience. Validate their emotions and let them know it's okay to make mistakes—that's how we learn and grow. You always want to be the one they know they can trust with how they're feeling. Offer guidance without being judgmental, and remind them of their strengths and the progress they've made. Celebrate their successes, no matter how small they may seem, to reinforce positive self-talk and resilience.

The Importance of Strong Family Relationships

As preteens navigate the challenges of growing up, a supportive and loving family environment provides a sense of security and belonging.

With strong family relationships, preteens are more likely to feel loved and accepted for who they are.

Healthy family relationships can also serve to help your preteen with relationships outside of the home. Modeling open communication, empathy, and forgiveness within the family sets a powerful example for interacting with others. Regularly sharing meals, having meaningful conversations, and engaging in activities together inside your home helps them to know how to do the same outside your home too.

With strong family relationships, preteens are also more likely to feel loved and accepted for who they are. This helps them be more self-confident and authentic, which helps them form healthy friendships. Strong relationships within families also help preteens' social lives because they are able to see healthy interactions and learn proper social skills by engaging with adults and children alike. By communicating openly, solving problems biblically, and showing empathy, you're equipping your child with the skills they need to develop strong relationships outside the walls of your home.

Sharing common interests with them and learning about what excites them also gives them the confidence that what they say matters. Those conversations you're having with them about their Legos, hobbies, favorite trading cards, and so on are actually providing them with practice in sharing those interests with others. That polish will go a long way as they chat with their friends about those things after church or as they play.

Having strong family relationships also helps our preteens know they have a safe place to open up about their thoughts and feelings. Open and caring conversations provide an open door for parents to help guide their preteen's faith journey or even discuss things like school, teams, and friends.

The Model for Lifelong, Caring Relationships

Engaged parents can also help their children navigate difficult or hurtful situations that may arise with others. In a study done by the American Psychological Association in which seventy-four fifth graders were evaluated, they found that "children who viewed their relationship with their mother as more secure were significantly more accepted by peers, had more reciprocated friendships, and were less lonely than children who rated the relationship as less secure."[16]

They also found that when they evaluated friendships between two children, there was a clear difference in the way they interacted with one another. The ones with a good relationship with their parents were less critical, more responsive, and found more companionship than the ones who had a strained relationship with parents. Helping your preteen build strong relationships within your family gives them a foundation for good relationship skills that will last a lifetime.

Just as strong, healthy family relationships influence our children's abilities to build relationships outside our families, a negative family dynamic can also have an impact on them, as we saw in the study mentioned above. Much of a child's emotional competence comes from within his family, so if your home is full of stress and conflict or if conversations within your family are strained and hurtful, you'll likely see the impact of that on your child's ability to have healthy friendships.

GUIDING YOUR CHILDREN'S RELATIONSHIPS

Leslie

The Bible makes it clear that the friendships we have are important. We see in Proverbs 12:26 that "The righteous choose their friends carefully, but the way of the wicked leads them astray." Proverbs 13:20 echoes that idea when Solomon writes, "Walk with the wise and become wise, for a companion of fools suffers harm."

Even the apostle Paul gave instructions to the church in Corinth about the way they chose their friends: "Do not be misled: Bad company corrupts good character" (1 Cor. 15:33). Our heavenly Father is concerned with the people we hang around with and call friends, so it's important for parents to help guide our children's relationships and give them principles they can use as they're choosing their companions.

Boys and Friends: Leslie

I have parented both boys and girls, and I assure you the way they approach friendships is not the same! In fact, when my boys were young, I was afraid they'd never have friends, and I certainly didn't understand the things they did together when I orchestrated times for them to play with other boys their age. Since I grew up with only a sister, I had no idea how boys functioned. My oldest son was my guinea pig not only in parenting but also in learning about boys in general.

One October, my oldest son, Camden, was turning nine, and I thought it was time to help him form a good core of friends. That's when I came up with one of the "best" ideas of my parenting career so far: a sleepover for nine- and ten-year-old boys. I was so excited to get to know some of the boys in Camden's class and to see them all have a great time together.

Because I wanted this to be successful and fun, I poured myself into preparing for the big event. We had lots of great food, Nerf guns for everyone, and a clean room where they could all throw down their sleeping bags in eager anticipation of an amazing night.

I wish I could say that calling the event a disaster was an overstatement, but it's not. Preteen boys can be painfully awkward and unbelievably loud. When you get a bunch of them together, they can destroy your stuff and each other before you know what's happening. By the next morning, I'm pretty sure they were all mortal enemies who hadn't slept much . . . and were ready for war. The one they called "Loopy" terrorized everyone, and my newly painted kitchen had a huge scrape on the wall. I learned some valuable lessons that day:

1. I can put my children in situations where they can build relationships with others that I believe would be good friends to them, but I can't orchestrate their interactions with one another —and when I do try to do that, it's generally really awkward and uncomfortable.

2. I can teach my children what to look for in friends and talk about the qualities they should possess and look for in others, but I ultimately have to allow them to find the ones they naturally gravitate toward without trying to force friendships or control their social circle.

3. I can create opportunities for my children to hang out with others, like game nights or opportunities to come to our home. I can get to know the kids they're hanging out with, so I can offer guidance if I have concerns about a particular friend or group.

And perhaps the most valuable lesson of all? That sleepovers with preteen boys is a recipe for a loud, long, destructive night and should probably be avoided!

As a parent, you have the opportunity to model healthy friendships. Giving boys the tools they need to comfortably start conversations with others and encouraging them to be loving and kind to the people around them goes a long way. One easy thing to relay is that having a good friend starts with being a good friend.

Girls and Friends: Tricia

As any parent of a preteen knows, girl friendships take on a whole new level of importance during these formative years. Suddenly, the seemingly simple dynamics of childhood playdates give way to complex webs of relationships, filled with both promise and potential pitfalls. Conversations that once centered around dolls or cartoons now revolve around boys, body changes, and social hierarchies.

These friendships become a training ground for navigating emotions, empathy, and conflict resolution—skills that will serve our daughters well throughout their lives. Yet, the intensity of preteen girl relationships can also bring challenges, from occasional drama and exclusion, to the constant comparison that social media fosters. We can help our daughters survive and thrive in this critical stage by offering guidance, open communication, and unconditional support.

When John and I bought our current home, we had no idea that one of the best features of our home was a built-in best friend for our youngest daughters. Our new next-door neighbors had two boys and a girl, and that girl, Preslie, was right in the middle of our daughters' ages.

I can't tell you how often those three girls zipped between the neighbor's house and ours. I'm actually surprised they didn't wear a path in the grass. There have been countless craft times, nail painting sessions, movie nights, and sleepovers. If my house seemed too quiet, I would text Preslie's mom to check on things because I knew that's where my girls must be.

While there were minor arguments, things ran smoothly with this threesome until they all started going through puberty. Oh, the drama! Things were said that hurt feelings seemingly every day during that season. For a while, two girls paired up against the other one. Then, the next week the alliances would switch.

There were even a few months when my two girls swore off friendship with their best friend, and although I tried to help them smooth things out, they were adamant that they would no longer be friends with her . . . until a few months later when they all made up and acted as if nothing happened. I got to the place where I would just nod and listen as they described the newest drama, having full faith that things would work out . . . and they did. Though Preslie's family has now moved to a new town twenty minutes away, the girls still spend regular time together. In my mind, they will have that "forever" type of friendship—the type where you just pick up where you left off even when you haven't seen each other for a while.

Of course, during the preteen years, Preslie wasn't their only friend. They've connected with other girls in co-ops, in youth groups, and at church. They've made friends at homeschool conferences, summer camps, and on cruises, but the truth is, girl friendships can be tough, especially these days. Trying to find good, solid friends is one of the things we've struggled with most.

In addition, there's drama. I can't count the number of times when my preteen girls found a new friend and things seemed to be going along well until suddenly they weren't. Girls can turn on girls quickly, and I've seen tears and confusion when a friend suddenly becomes a bully. I've talked with my girls and prayed with them about this. I've also given them hope that things aren't quite so hard when they get older.

As older teens and adults, we find friends in new ways: through our hobbies or work. Or at church and Bible study. I have good friends of all ages, yet that's harder to figure out as a preteen. They're in the awkward middle. Kids younger than them are still into toys and make-believe, while older girls already in their early and mid-teens are often into clothes, guys, and talking about starting jobs and learning to drive. And so, for a season, preteens look to other preteens for friendships—and with everyone emotional or hormonal, there are a lot of ups and downs!

I offer myself as a BFF when other girls aren't the best option.

Over the years, I've learned to help my girls by doing my best to take them on outings and include friends to come along. We have friends over, and we allow our daughters to hang out in the homes of families we trust, but we've also decided sleepovers aren't a good idea. Those are just too many hours for things to go south. What usually starts out as a good time often turns into someone upset at someone else for things that were said.

I also make an effort to spend time with my girls more. We like to thrift for clothes and visit vintage markets. They're always up for a coffee date or smoothie run. We like to travel and plan activities. I offer myself as a BFF when other girls aren't the best option. That doesn't mean I'm not a parent. I am. But I also create lots of opportunities for fun so my preteen girls aren't just sitting at home and feeling left out.

A Laboratory for Social Skills

For boys and girls alike, preteen friendships help shape their sense of self and provide a laboratory for social skills. Yet, the nature of boy friendships and girl friendships often differs in some key ways.

As Leslie mentioned, for boys, friendships are frequently activity-based. Think video games, pickup basketball, or simply hanging out in the neighborhood. These shared pursuits provide a framework for bonding. Social hierarchies can emerge, with certain kids taking on leadership roles, but within that structure, there's room for camaraderie and shared adventures. While boys might not always express their friendships through open displays of affection, the connections they form are real and meaningful.

On the flip side, preteen girls often invest deeply in their friendships on an emotional level. Conversations can revolve around relationships, feelings, and shared secrets. As I've seen over and over, alliances might shift as different girls connect and clash. While drama can be a part of the equation, these friendships also offer girls a chance to explore empathy, support, and mutual understanding, not to mention forgiveness!

It's essential for parents to recognize that both boy- and girl-styles of friendship have value. By supporting our preteens as they navigate these relationships, we help them build social skills, resilience, and a sense of belonging. Whether your child is a sports-loving boy or a drama-enthusiast girl, their friendships play a pivotal role in the preteen journey.

Quick Take on Boys and Girls

Boys

- **Action-oriented:** Friendships are often centered around activities, games, and adventures. Think video games, sports, and roughhousing.

- **Hierarchical:** Cliques and social hierarchies are common, with popular kids leading the pack. There can be a competitive edge to their friendships.

- **Rule-based:** Games and activities come with rules, and boys often enjoy the structure and boundaries these provide.

- **Emotionally reserved:** Open displays of affection are less common. Boys might show friendship through teasing or playful jabs rather than hugs or heartfelt talks.

- **Larger groups:** Boy friendships often occur in bigger groups, like a whole sports team or a cluster of kids united by a shared interest.

Girls

- **Emotionally intense:** Preteen girls invest deeply in their friendships. Conversations can be long, personal, and filled with drama.

- **Relationally complex:** Alliances can shift quickly, and social dynamics can feel like a roller coaster. Think inside jokes, secrets, and occasional fallouts.

- **One-on-one focused:** Girls who participate in groups often have a best friend and prioritize those one-on-one bonds.

- **Appearance matters:** Style, looks, and fitting into certain aesthetics can influence friendships.

- **Gossip-prone:** With a focus on relationships and social standing, gossip (both harmless and hurtful) can be a part of the girl friendship landscape.

Important Note: It's crucial to remember that these are generalizations. Many boys have emotionally deep friendships, and many girls thrive in competitive, action-oriented groups. But as a parent, these generalizations have helped me to understand these relationships better. Through the ups and downs of preteen friendships, I've learned not to get too stressed—or too involved. We can be guides, but it's important that kids learn how to work out these relationships and develop the skills for ones in the future.

RELATIONSHIPS WITHIN GROUPS

Tricia

While one-on-one relationships are essential, it is also important for preteens to foster connections in groups and with people of all ages. Relationships with church members and community members can significantly impact your preteen's faith journey. People who have been most impactful in my children's spiritual growth have been other godly adults who have taken the time to go to coffee with one of my children or teach them in youth group.

My oldest daughter, Leslie Joy, had an amazing homeschool basketball coach. "Coachie" had a daughter on the team and he spent just as much time talking about character and godly living as he did teaching them how to dribble and shoot. My daughter still talks about him with fondness to this day. These types of relationships provide additional support, mentorship, and a sense of community, reinforcing the values and teachings they receive at home.

Community involvement is another avenue for preteens to develop meaningful relationships and grow their faith. As mentioned previously, encourage your preteens to participate in community service projects, local sports teams, or hobby groups. Engaging with the community teaches preteens the importance of service, compassion, and being a positive influence in the world.

Community or service activities not only help preteens build social skills but also expose them to diverse perspectives, which is another opportunity for growth. We can spend time with others who don't believe as we do, and show them that we care. These interactions can lead to great conversations.

I've had countless talks with my preteens as we've driven home from serving, especially after leaving the teen mom support group I previously led. My daughters overheard a lot, and while I first questioned if they were becoming aware of too much, I discovered instead that they were seeing firsthand how our decisions impact every part of our lives. God's Word gives us directives for godly living, not to keep us from having fun, but to guide us toward the abundant, joyful living that God has designed for His children.

Investing in the Lives of Other Preteens

While our children are preteens for a season, it's important to invest in the lives of other preteens as well. Recently, I was spending time with friends and their three daughters, ages eight to fifteen. With a loss in their family, the girls have more emotional days than not. Attempting to bring some fun into the grayness, I asked eleven-year-old Ella if she wanted to create a TikTok dance with me. We did, and we had so much fun! As I speak around the country, I often teach that same dance to attendees for fun during our breaks or before a session starts. I also make sure to record it and send it to Ella. It always brightens her day!

These small moments can have a lasting impact. As I mentioned earlier, my Sunday school teacher, Margo, took us out to lunch to memorize Scripture verses when I was a preteen. It was a simple act, but it left a lasting impression on me. These experiences strengthen preteen relationships and create lasting bonds and cherished memories.

LET OTHERS INVEST IN YOUR CHILDREN
Leslie

As Tricia has shown, involving your children in community activities helps them build great relationships with others. Being part of a church family also offers your preteens a broader support network. Community involvement allows them to interact with godly men and women who can serve as role models and mentors. Encourage your preteens to participate in church events, volunteer opportunities, and mission trips along with you. These experiences can deepen their faith and broaden their perspective in wonderful ways.

When my kids were younger, we were part of a church plant. They helped set up and tear down chairs, working side by side with other members of our church body in this and other multigenerational tasks. Now that my kids are adults, they still maintain relationships with those older church members. They have prayed and served together, and these godly men and women, whom they now call friends, continue investing in their lives.

* * *

When you engage in service and community activities as a family, your children see you setting an example, but they also build relationships with various godly men and women. These relationships can have a lasting impact, reinforcing the values and teachings you instill at home. Other adults in your community can invest in your children in ways that complement and enhance your own influence. This network of support and mentorship helps nurture your children's faith and character, providing them with additional role models and sources of wisdom and guidance.

Chapter Twelve

CREATE A POSITIVE AND WELCOMING HOME ENVIRONMENT

Making and Cherishing Memories

Who do you like to spend the most time with? Where do you like to hang out? It's easy to say that we want to be the place where our kids enjoy having friends. Or the place where they can just be themselves, knowing they're loved for who they are, flaws and all. It takes both a positive and welcoming environment to make that happen.

WELCOME AT HOME

Tricia

I've learned a lot about what it means to truly have a "welcome home" over the years. When my older kids were little, I often got stressed over the messes—the toys scattered everywhere, the dirty dishes left in the sink, and the endless piles of laundry. The clutter felt like chaos, and I tried to control it. But with our adopted kids, I noticed something deeper. I found myself slipping into the role of a mom trying to "fix all the things," as if managing behavior and orchestrating schedules could create peace and connection. But I missed the bigger picture: Our home wasn't meant to be a place of orderliness. It was meant to be a place of belonging. Let's pause for a moment and talk about the difference between having a positive home and a welcoming home.

A positive home environment is a place where love and respect are consistently shown. It's vital for building strong family relationships with preteens. But a welcoming home? That goes even deeper. A welcoming home isn't just about rules or routines. It's about creating a space where hearts are nurtured and there's room for messiness—not just in the living room but also in our relationships. It's where preteens feel free to be themselves, to share their thoughts and feelings without fear of judgment.

In a welcoming home, we don't rush to fix things. Instead, we lean into the mess, knowing that true growth happens in those moments of connection. It's not about managing behavior, it's about building trust. That's the environment where faith takes root, where kids see grace in action. It's where they learn they don't have to be perfect to be loved. And that all of us make mistakes, but we can grow together.

Of course, this is something I learned after making a lot of mistakes. I didn't realize at the time my efforts to "get my kids ready for life" were putting a wedge in our relationship. How? As my children transitioned from kid to preteen, it was as if a switch went off in my mind. It was as if there was a countdown, and there were things I needed to do to prepare them to launch as adults.

A Winning Strategy

One of the big switches happened when my kids turned twelve, and they got promoted to the "big chore chart." At that time, chores moved from keeping their room clean and taking out the trash to having kitchen, living room, or bathroom duty one day a week.

It wasn't fun for preteens to have new responsibilities, but one of our daughters had an especially hard time. She'd whine and complain whenever it was her turn to do the chores. And sometimes, the conflicts were bigger than that. There were days when getting her to do her chores almost seemed like a battle of wits and will.

I tried different things to give consequences to grumbling kids. One thing I tried was having a Gratitude Jar. Every time the kids complained, they first had to write a letter of gratitude.

I tried it out with this daughter, who again grumbled about having to do her kitchen chores.

"Fine, I'll do the dumb kitchen," she complained.

"Thank you, but you must also write a gratitude first."

"This is stupid."

"That sounds like a grumble. Make that two gratitudes."

She stomped out of the room, calling back over her shoulder, "I'm not going to write anything for your dumb jar."

"That makes three gratitudes."

Her grumbling continued all the way down the stairs, and by the time we arrived in the kitchen, she was up to nine. Obviously, that strategy didn't work.

A few days later, I was praying about the complaining, and God stirred my heart.

Why would she want to do her chores?

I thought about our most recent interactions. When she finally got around to cleaning the kitchen, she'd do it halfway, and then I'd point out what needed to be done better. In my mind, I was training her. In her mind, I was being too picky. No, it wasn't fun for her at all.

"What should I do instead?" I prayed.

An answer immediately filled my mind: "Praise her."

So that's what I did. The next time she cleaned the kitchen, I made it a point to walk through it and point out everything she was doing right. I continued to do that over the next fifteen minutes as I took that path to carry laundry baskets to the bedrooms. And the thing was, the more I praised, the more she cleaned. Forty-five minutes later, the whole kitchen shone, and you can believe I really praised her then. I even told John that night what a fantastic job she'd done on her chore.

So, for months, praise became my go-to response, and to this day, out of all of our kids, she's the best at cleaning the kitchen. I'm so thankful I asked God for help. Sometimes, the little things—such as shifts in our own attitudes—change everything.

A Smile, Soft Voice, and Clear Requests

Raising preteens is an education for parents. While my daughter Maria was always easygoing, as I got to know her, I discovered that when she was too quiet, something was going on. I knew then to take some time to be with her and figure out what was going on.

Our twins, who were twelve years old when we adopted them, were just the opposite. Loud and confrontational, anyone knew exactly what was happening in their heads because they let you know. The first few years after their adoption, there was so much conflict between them (and between them and everyone else) that I often found myself tensing up when they entered the room. Again, I prayed that God would show me how to parent them better. His message to my heart was simple: soften up. I knew what He meant. Soften my attitude. Soften my scowl. Soften my tone. Soften my stance.

God's message was simple: soften up. I started by taking deep breaths and relaxing my tense shoulders.

Because the twins were so challenging, I easily became rigid and edgy when they were around. While I'm a very chill and relaxed person (most of the time), my attitude flips when I feel under stress. Sometimes, my forehead would be furrowed in concentration as I thought of the book I was working on, and my adopted preteens would think I was angry with them. Other times, when something needed to be done quickly, my voice rose an octave, and I became serious about the job at hand.

In the chaos of parenting preteens, it's easy to get caught up in the daily struggles and busy schedules and become tense or unyielding. We often forget that we don't have to be caught up in the overwhelm. Instead, here are a few simple yet powerful ways we can connect with our children—even during those times.

To soften up, I started by taking deep breaths and relaxing my tense shoulders. I also worked to incorporate softer habits. By making a few intentional shifts in our approach, we can ease tensions, open lines of communication, and build stronger, more loving relationships with our kids. Here are a few great places to start:

SMILE: A smile is more than just a facial expression. When we smile at our children, we're sending a powerful message of love, acceptance, and safety. Our smile has the ability to ease our child's worries, calm their fears, and break down the walls they may put up as they navigate the challenges of preteen years. By making a conscious effort to smile at our child whenever we make eye contact—as we greet them in the morning, as we see them throughout the day—we're creating a warm and welcoming environment that invites them to open up to us.

SPEAK SOFTLY: We've all experienced the escalating cycle of raising our voices as our kids get louder. But what if we could break that cycle by doing the opposite? By speaking softly to our children, we can create a calming atmosphere, encouraging them to respond in kind. Whether we're asking about their day or requesting they put away their belongings, approaching them with a soft and gentle voice can help de-escalate tensions and make them more receptive to our requests. The next time the volume in your home starts to rise, try lowering yours instead. You may be surprised at how quickly the atmosphere can shift.

CLARITY OVER CLEVERNESS: It's easy to fall into the trap of beating around the bush when communicating with our kids, often in an effort to avoid conflict or confrontation. But indirect language can lead to confusion and make our children question whether we're truly serious about our requests.

We can eliminate confusion and clarify their expectations by saying exactly what we mean in a kind but firm manner. Instead of asking, "Why is this room a mess?" we can say, "Please pick up your games and books and put them away in their proper places." By being as specific as possible, we can help our children understand our expectations and take ownership of meeting them.

LET GO OF EXPECTATIONS: Before our children were born (or adopted!), we likely had visions of who they would be and how they would behave. But our kids are unique individuals with their own personalities, strengths, and weaknesses. By surrendering our preconceived notions of who they should be, we can make space to love and accept them for who they are. This doesn't mean we abandon our role of guiding them and teaching them right from wrong. But it does mean we let go of the stress and tension that comes from trying to mold them into someone they're not. By embracing their individuality and celebrating their unique gifts, we can build a stronger, more loving relationship that will last a lifetime.

We can create a more peaceful and loving home environment by implementing these simple yet powerful practices—smiling, speaking softly, being clear and direct, letting go of expectations, as well as asking for help. We can break down the walls that often come up in the preteen years and build a strong foundation for the years to come.

A WELCOME HOME THAT STAYS WITH OUR CHILDREN

As we journey alongside our preteens in their faith, it is essential to celebrate their progress and accomplishments while seeking opportunities to share their journey with others. Even when faced with challenges, maintaining a positive attitude and staying close to our preteens is crucial.

Recognize that they are on their unique faith journey, and trust in God's plan for their lives. Though investing in their faith may take time, stay committed, knowing that the rewards will come in the years ahead.

Legacy

Take the time to acknowledge and celebrate each step and milestone your preteen achieves in their faith journey. Share these moments with family, friends, and your faith community. Celebrations not only reinforce their efforts but also encourage them to continue growing in their faith.

Years ago, I (Leslie) read an article about an older woman who journaled in Bibles to give to young moms and teens in her church. I thought that was an amazing concept. So when my oldest was around twelve, I started a tradition of creating Legacy Bibles for each of my children. I thought I would read through God's Word with one of my children in mind and journal my thoughts, experiences, hopes for them, prayers for their future, and more. I wanted to present the Bibles to them on their sixteenth birthday. (Tricia and I also wrote a book about *How to Create a Legacy Bible* together since we discovered we were each doing something similar for our children.)

As I was nearing the end of Camden's Bible, I started thinking about all the other men and women God had put in his life that had made an impact. These godly individuals had seen him grow both physically and spiritually through the years, and I wanted to allow them to share their thoughts and prayers with him as well, so for about a month before his sixteenth birthday, I secretly passed his new Bible around to our pastor and others in the church, as well as allowing my parents and sister to write in it. They remembered things about him I had totally forgotten, and it was humbling to see how much thought they took in sharing with him in their inscriptions. When it was finally time to hand it over, I was thrilled to see his excitement at receiving it.

I've created Legacy Bibles for all my children and am working on my daughter-in-law's edition as this book is being written. Those Bibles give my children an heirloom quality look at their mom's hopes for them, the lessons their dad and I have learned, and how I've seen them grow throughout their lives. My prayer is that it will always serve as a physical reminder of the faithfulness of God to them and to our family.

Traditions to Make Memories

Like Leslie, I (Tricia) love creating Legacy Bibles for my kids! I've finished six, and I have four to go. I love the idea that my children will always have their Bibles with the prayers I prayed and the encouragement I gave. It's also important to me to build family traditions.

> **Ditch the perfect tradition myth. Things won't always go as planned.**

Sticking to these traditions, even during the preteen years, is crucial. God has called us to go for the hearts of our kids, and there's no pause button on that. Maintaining these traditions and expectations helps children rise to the occasion and appreciate the value of these moments.

For years, I felt overwhelmed by the pressure to create perfect holidays for my family. I'd spend hours planning and preparing, only to feel stressed and exhausted. I realized I didn't have to let the chaos of special days steal the joy from our time together. Here's how I found a better way to create traditions that my preteens love, all year round:

Pick a few traditions and make them special. Trying to do everything drains the fun out of special days. By choosing just a few traditions that my kids love, we can really enjoy them. We have a yearly ritual to set up the Christmas tree on Thanksgiving weekend to kick off the holiday season. On birthdays, the birthday child gets a one-on-one date with Mom and Dad at the restaurant of their choice. Focusing on a few things that bring us joy makes special days feel more relaxed and fun.

Ditch the perfect tradition myth. Let's face it: preteens can be messy and moody. Things won't always go as planned. Your kid might roll their eyes at the dinner table. That's okay! Lower your expectations and laugh off the imperfections. What matters most is that you're making time for each other and creating memories.

Spend time, not money. Preteens care more about your attention than your gift-giving skills. Instead of stressing over finding the perfect present, spend that time doing something fun together. Go for a hike, play a game, or try a new recipe. Get creative and make something together—it doesn't have to be perfect! Those are the memories they'll carry with them.

Make it about more than just holidays. There are special moments all year round. Find ways to make "everyday" days feel exciting. Create traditions around things like the first day of school (we take a photo in the same spot every year), the start of summer (we have a backyard BBQ), or the end of the school year (we write down our favorite memories from the year). It spreads joy throughout the year and makes the ordinary feel special.

Also, involve them in the planning. Preteens want to be heard. Ask your kids what they want to do to celebrate special days. Do they have a favorite activity or tradition? Let them take the lead on planning that part of your celebration. They'll be more invested and excited about the things they choose. And who knows, you might just start a new favorite tradition, and it's especially fun to see adult children carry these traditions into their families!

A FAITH THAT LASTS

Tricia

Sometimes, it gets so easy to focus on the now that we lose sight of what we're striving for. One of the benefits of parenting ten children is having kids in middle school and knowing what to focus on and what not to worry about. While the older kids insist I'm more relaxed with the younger kids, I've realized that I don't need to stress over everything. In fact, the more I focus on guiding my children's faith journey, the less I have to worry so much about all the other things. If a child has a strong faith, then they will seek the Lord. They will also heed the Holy Spirit. When children seek God as they grow, they will make better decisions stemming from a desire to please God, not just because Mom and Dad say so. A welcoming home, peaceful environment, and family traditions aren't just for today. They are also for the future. Seeing the seeds of faith we planted in our kids grow and flourish makes all the time and intention worth it.

Another joy of having adult children is hearing their stories about their childhood. When my adult kids get together, they often tell tales of adventures and mishaps I never knew about. They laugh and reminisce, and these shared memories bind them together. God, in His grace, kept them safe through it all, and now they have these wonderful stories to look back on.

Seeing your children grow into adults who love God can be a reward. There's a sense of pride and peace in knowing that the values and faith you instilled in them have taken root. The adult years are filled with joy as you enjoy your kids without the constant need for discipline. You get to appreciate them as individuals with their own interests and passions.

My older kids are often at our house, and the time we spent reading together has come full circle as we now write novels together. We'll spend hours brainstorming stories, sharing our writing, and offering feedback. It's amazing to see the creativity and talent they bring to our collaborations. My daughter in the Czech Republic and my oldest son are now reading the Chronicles of Narnia to their kids, continuing the traditions we started. Hearing about them sharing these beloved books with the next generation brings so much joy.

*   *   *

The fun and depth of relationships that started in the preteen years can grow in the adult years. You get to be a part of their big decisions, like choosing a career path or getting married. You become a source of wisdom and guidance as they navigate the ups and downs of adulthood. And through it all, you get to enjoy them as friends, sharing laughs and making new memories together.

The adult years with your kids can be a reward for all the hard work of raising them, especially when their faith has stuck firm. Looking back, the little things really do matter. Taking time to create a positive and welcoming home is something you will be thankful for for decades to come.

Chapter Thirteen

KEEP THE FLAME ALIVE

Maintaining Momentum on Your Preteen's Faith Journey

I nvesting in your preteen's faith journey is a long-term commitment that requires patience, love, and trust in God's plan. By celebrating their progress, staying close, trusting in God's direction, and continuously loving and supporting them, you lay the groundwork for a resilient and enduring faith. As you journey together, rely on God's grace and guidance, knowing that your efforts will bear fruit in the years to come.

THE COOKIE PACT AND OTHER ANTICS

Leslie

One evening, as seven of the eight of us sat together at the dinner table recently, I learned about the cookie pact that my first and third children came up with when they were younger to cheat their siblings out of cookies.

It all started when Camden caught Lizzie Gray sneaking some cookie dough while she was making cookies. Realizing he'd caught her red-handed, they hatched a plan where he wouldn't mention her unbaked snack if she'd keep some dough out for him each time she made cookies. Then, when the baked cookies were handed out, Payton and

Lila would get one less cookie than everyone else, because they'd be given misinformation about how many they were allocated. Camden and Lizzie Gray were laughing like crazy, recounting the way the cookie pact came to be as Payton was coming to the stunning realization that he and Lila are owed *a lot* of cookies after all these years.

It seems like every time we're together, the kids unveil a new revelation of the things I never knew about. They seem to think the statute of limitations for their questionable behavior has passed, so they speak quite freely of the adventures they had and the stunts they pulled. I already knew about some of their biggest misadventures—the flamethrower they tested in the closed garage, the indoor skate ramp they created in the boys' room, the pool they tried to dig in the woods behind our house, and other antics that prove that God's hand is clearly on them since they survived their adolescence.

Not Perfect Parents

I'm so grateful that all my children still live close by. We get together regularly, and the stories they share and the way they laugh as they do mean the world to me. I've marveled at what's missing as they've reminisced together time after time. They talk about the trips we've taken, the shenanigans they did together, the injuries, the jokes, and more, but they don't talk about so many of the things I worried about through the years, the failures I grieved over so much. When they do bring up my "not finer moments" as a mom, they usually do so with the same kind of laughter they share over their own silly missteps. What they remember is the love they got from David and me. They remember the time we spent with them when they were pretty sure we had other things to do, and they remember how we sacrificed so they could have opportunities. (I know because they talk about it.) Having adult kids is amazing. A win-win, a 10 out of 10—I highly recommend!

David and I weren't perfect parents any more than you can be, but

God sure was faithful to take the little knowledge and lots of love we had to offer Him and use it for His glory and for the good of our family. He answered prayers every single day. He grew our own faith as we sought His will for parenting our children. He gave us ideas that turned out to be incredible for shaping

God gave us ideas that turned out to be incredible for shaping their faith and lives.

their faith and lives, and He created a family legacy of faith that we praise Him for as we pray together before bed almost every night.

To give your preteens a faith that sticks doesn't take perfect parenting. It's not contingent on knowing all the answers or coming up with all the right ideas at the right time. Giving your preteens a faith that sticks happens by the grace of God as an overflow of the faith that's growing in you each day. The old saying "More is caught than taught" makes sense, as your children will learn more from watching how you live than from anything you say. You can't teach your children biblical truths and life lessons you don't know yourself, and you can't reproduce in them a vibrant faith you don't have. Kids are incredibly perceptive, and they can see through the fakes pretty quickly.

But your children are also unbelievably gracious and forgiving when they see you sincerely trying. I can't begin to tell you how many times I've gone to my children to admit I blew it. I lost my temper. I made assumptions about them that were unfair and untrue and was blunt and gruff toward them because of it. I asked them to do things that, in hindsight, were too hard or too awkward for them and put them in difficult situations. I messed up plenty, but I always tried to ensure I didn't let anything fester that could cause a crack in our relationship.

The Importance of "I'm Sorry"

David stormed into Camden's room, the sound of our son's disrespect still echoing in his ears. "Camden, what's gotten into you?"

he yelled. Eleven-year-old Camden looked up and then quickly looked away.

"Dad, it wasn't my fault," Camden began, but David cut him off. "I don't want to hear your excuses," he snapped. Camden's face fell, and he clamped his mouth shut, his jaw jutting out. He dropped his gaze to the floor, his thin shoulders slumping as he sank onto the edge of his bed.

David stood over him. "You need to understand that your attitude is not okay," he lectured, trying to keep his tone firm but feeling a pang of guilt at the sight of his son's downcast face. "You can't talk to your mother like that. Do you hear me?" He paused, studying Camden's dejected posture and tears. "You need to get your act together, Camden." The room was silent except for the heavy weight of his words.

Feeling a wave of regret wash over him, David turned and strode from the room, leaving his son to his thoughts.

He left Cam in his room for a little while to cool down. Shortly thereafter, David returned to the room. Cam didn't glance up.

"Son." David's voice was gentle now. "I'm sorry." He didn't justify the reason he yelled or remind Camden that it was his attitude that had started it all. David simply told him that he was very sorry for raising his voice in a way that tore his son down. He asked for Camden's forgiveness.

David apologized, understanding that forgiveness is the way forward. As God teaches, forgiveness releases not only the wrongdoer but also the one wronged. Sometimes, saying sorry is the most powerful path to move forward.

In parenting, you are going to mess up. You aren't going to handle every punishment and circumstance with perfect consistency, justice, the right measure of grace, and wisdom. But to allow anger or bitterness to rise up will breach the relationship with your children, making it impossible to reach them, disciple, mentor, and direct them. If your children are holding on to anger or bitterness, it doesn't matter if you feel you're right. The way forward is to humble yourself and apologize for your reactions.

"Sorry" is a crucial word in discipling your children and building a faith that endures. Mistakes are inevitable, but apologizing to your kids doesn't diminish your authority. It demonstrates the repentance and humility that God desires (Heb. 12:15). By doing so, you model a faith that will stick and keep relationships healthy, avoiding the bitterness that can destroy their spiritual journey.

FOUNDATION FOR A FAITH THAT STICKS
Tricia

During this season of their lives, many preteens have very tender consciences. They may be deeply affected by their actions and seek guidance. Because of the relationships you've built, they will come to you, trusting you to help them navigate their feelings and choices. This relational foundation gives you countless opportunities to speak truth into their lives, providing the antidote to their struggles and guiding them according to God's Word. By being a consistent and loving presence, you help them build a faith that will endure throughout their lives.

Don't Rush Past Repentance

We have ten kids with ten different sin struggles. Then you add mine and John's sinful hearts, and just imagine how often people hurt, anger, and provoke each other in a day. Some kids' sins are more pronounced and visible. Yet sin is sin.

Of all my kids, my third oldest, Nathan, is the most amicable. He gets along with everyone and has a tender heart. At one gathering, my older kids were telling about everything they got in trouble for. There were things I'd forgotten. There were wrongs I should have been less concerned about. There were sin-struggles I should have paid more attention to. In the middle of the jesting, I commented, "All of you were a lot of work," I laughed, "except for Nathan—he didn't do anything wrong."

I was sort of joking and sort of not. Compared to some of the other kids, Nathan was a walk in the park. But as I looked over at Nathan his face was grim.

"What's wrong?" I asked.

"Mom, I have something to confess."

My stomach knotted up. "Okay . . ." My heartbeat quickened. I looked around as everyone quieted to hear.

"Mom, when I was eleven or twelve, and you told me to go to bed." He paused and continued. "Well, I used to sneak in my Game Boy and play until late. That's why I was sometimes tired for school the next day."

Relieved laughter spilled out of my lips. That was all? But he was serious, and I could tell this had been bothering him for a while.

> **When we guide our children in God's ways, they will be changed. The amazing thing is that we're changed too.**

"I forgive you, Nathan, for disobeying me. Thank you for letting me know."

Even though Nathan was in his twenties at the time, that sin of disobedience had bothered him. Accepting my forgiveness brought a smile.

Nathan still has a tender heart. Tonight at dinner, we were talking about a card game we'd played the night before. Nathan had misread one of the cards, and he couldn't use the strategy he had planned on to win the game. Because of that, he lost by a lot.

I laughed and commented. "You know, none of us read that card right. We never would have known."

"But I would have," he said. And that caused my heart to double in two. Whether my children have big or small struggles, the guidance we give, the verses we memorize, and the prayers we pray will have an impact. Even when we're gone, the legacy of faith we offered will live on. I know that now. And it encourages me to be even more intentional with our younger kids. Casey and Alyssa are fourteen. We're still on the journey, and I'm excited about the path.

When we guide our children in God's ways and give them our love, attention, care, and time, they will be changed. The amazing thing is that we're changed too. I'm a different mom now than when my oldest son entered the preteen years. To teach and guide, we need to follow God first.

I see the challenges differently now. I see these challenges as *my* path, leading me closer to God. As I lean in, seeking God's guidance and strength, I learn to depend on Him step by step. As I navigate the preteen years, I'm growing in faith, patience, and wisdom, becoming the parent my children need.

Building a strong faith foundation during their preteen years equips your children to face life's challenges with resilience and confidence. Teach them to rely on God's promises and to seek His guidance in difficult times. By fostering a deep and personal relationship with God early on, they develop a source of strength and comfort that will sustain them throughout their lives. And as we walk this journey alongside them, we too are strengthened, our roots of faith deepening with each step.

JUST THE BEGINNING

As preteens transition into adolescence and adulthood, it's important to recognize that this is not the end of their faith journey but rather the beginning of a new phase. This period is filled with growth, challenges, and opportunities for deepening their relationship with God. Understanding that their faith journey continues to evolve helps set the stage for ongoing spiritual development.

Keeping your family's faith journey centered on God and His plan is paramount. Regularly remind your preteen of God's love, purpose, and promises. Encourage them to trust in His plan for their life, even when the path seems uncertain. This focus helps them to navigate challenges with a sense of purpose and divine direction.

Stay positive and continue to love and support your preteen throughout this journey. Your unwavering support and encouragement are essential as they navigate the ups and downs of adolescence. Trust that God has a plan for their faith journey, and remain confident that your efforts to help them grow will pay off.

By recognizing that the preteen years are just the beginning of a lifelong faith journey, and by staying connected and investing in their spiritual growth, you can help your child develop a strong, enduring faith. Through prayer, Bible study, deep conversations, and the support of your faith community, you can guide them through the challenges of adolescence and prepare them for a future grounded in God's love and purpose.

Continue to Invest

Understand that your preteen is on their unique faith journey, and trust that God has a plan for their life. There will be times when their path diverges from what you expected, but faith means trusting in God's greater plan. Stay positive and keep going, knowing your investment in your preteen's faith will pay off in the coming years. Embrace the journey with an open heart, confident that God guides you and your child.

Throughout this book, we've learned more about our preteens— how they think, how they're developing, and how we can effectively reach their hearts.

Above all, continue to love and support your teen. Your unwavering love and commitment provide the security they need to explore and grow in their faith. Trust in God's grace and direction as you go through life together. Be there to listen, guide, and encourage them every step of the way. Your presence and support will help them build a resilient and enduring faith.

When I (Leslie) was young, my dad, in

an attempt to be funny, came home one afternoon with a book he found on his travels: *How to Get a Preteen to Run Away from Home*. I had totally forgotten about that silly book until I started working on this project and found it on a shelf in my parents' house. It details a lot of stereotypical ways parents can get on their children's nerves and make them want to escape the torture of their home as soon as possible. (It also included some wildly inappropriate torture techniques that made me pretty sure Dad saw the cover and thought it was funny, but that he never looked through the book before giving it to me!)

Clearly, parents have struggled to know how to deal with their adolescents for a long time. As parents on a mission, though, the last thing we want to do is sever relationships with our children or be a stumbling block to them as they grow in their faith.

Throughout this book, we've learned more about our preteens—how they think, how they're developing, and how we can effectively reach their hearts. Tricia and I hope that removes the mystery about how to approach them and makes you excited about the new and more mature ways you can start to disciple them. It's been so fun for me to think back to those days and remember with joy much of what we experienced.

I've also been reminded of how grateful I am that God led us through that stage and the teen years as well, to relentlessly go for our children's hearts and do all we could to give them a solid foundation for a faith that sticks. God has been so faithful to bless the simple offering we had to give as parents.

* * *

We pray that you are encouraged that parenting and disciplining your preteens well is attainable and can be enjoyable. You've been teaching them well through all the stages of their lives so far, and you're perfectly equipped to lead them through this one with tender, loving care, too. Stay engaged. Let them know you're in their corner and that you are their greatest advocate and cheerleader as they grow. And, most importantly, point them to Jesus every chance you can. Model for them a life of holiness and devotion, and give them the tools they need to build their own life of faith as well.

Giving your children a faith that sticks should be a natural overflow of your own growing faith. As you model a vibrant relationship with God, you'll equip your children with the spiritual tools they need to navigate life's challenges. By growing together, you'll not only strengthen your family bonds but also raise the next generation of believers who will make a difference in the world.

* * *

A PRAYER FOR YOU AND YOUR PRETEEN

Dear Lord, I ask for Your wisdom and guidance as I navigate this preteen stage with my child. Help me be an active participant in their faith journey, not just a spectator on the sidelines. Give me the strength and patience to set healthy boundaries while spending quality time together. I pray for understanding as they navigate the ups and downs of preteen development and search for their identity. Be the bedrock of our family, providing faith and stability amidst the chaos.

As emotions run high, teach me to validate their feelings while pointing them to You as our ultimate comfort. Ignite a passion in their heart for prayer, that it may be the lifeblood of their faith. Stir in them a hunger for Your Word, making the Bible come alive in their life. Give us meaningful conversations and deep connections as we explore Scripture together. Help me listen well so that I might truly hear their heart and spark open dialogue.

Grant me words of eternal impact as I have intentional spiritual conversations. Show us how to be Your hands and feet, serving others and showcasing Your love. As they branch out, help them build strong, godly relationships that encourage their faith. Create a warm and welcoming home environment where memories are made and cherished.

Most of all, Lord, work in their lives to keep the flame of their faith burning bright. Give me the creativity and perseverance to maintain momentum on this journey. I pray that as they grow, their roots of faith will run deep, anchoring them in You. May they come to know You more and more, and may our bond as parent and child be strengthened through the gift of showing up. In Jesus' name, amen.

SCRIPTURE TREASURY

Below is a list of Scripture verses about identity, worth, and other topics we've talked about.[17] These verses provide a helpful guide to praying Scriptures with your children.

May they know the Scriptures, which are able to make them wise for salvation

2 Timothy 3:15: "From childhood you have been acquainted with the sacred writings, which are able to make you wise for salvation through faith in Christ Jesus."

May they come to know Christ as personal Savior

2 Peter 3:9: "The Lord is not slow to fulfill his promise as some count slowness, but is patient toward you, not wishing that any should perish, but that all should reach repentance."

May they know God and serve Him

1 Chronicles 28:9: "Know the God of your father and serve him with a whole heart and with a willing mind, for the LORD searches all hearts and understands every plan and thought. If you seek him, he will be found by you, but if you forsake him, he will cast you off forever."

May they grow in the grace and knowledge of Jesus Christ

2 Peter 3:18: "But grow in the grace and knowledge of our Lord and Savior Jesus Christ. To him be the glory both now and to the day of eternity. Amen."

May they be obedient to parents

Ephesians 6:1: "Children, obey your parents in the Lord, for this is right."

May they be respectful to parents

Ephesians 6:2: "Honor your father and mother (this is the first commandment with a promise)."

May they have a heart for God

Deuteronomy 5:29: "Oh that they had such a heart as this always, to fear me and to keep all my commandments, that it might go well with them and with their descendants forever!"

May they hate sin

Psalms 97:10: "O you who love the LORD, hate evil!"

May they understand their sin will be found out

Numbers 32:23: "Be sure your sin will find you out."

May they be quick to repent

Psalms 32:1: "Blessed is the one whose transgression is forgiven, whose sin is covered."

May they be quick to forgive

Ephesians 4:32: "Be kind to one another, tenderhearted, forgiving one another, as God in Christ forgave you."

May they choose the right friends

Proverbs 13:20: "Whoever walks with the wise becomes wise, but the companion of fools will suffer harm."

1 Corinthians 15:33: "Do not be deceived: 'Bad company ruins good morals.'"

May they say no to sin

Proverbs 1:10: "If sinners entice you, do not consent."

May they learn to submit to God

James 4:7: "Submit yourselves therefore to God. Resist the devil, and he will flee from you."

May they have a repentant heart

Psalms 51:1–3: "Have mercy on me, O God, according to your steadfast love; according to your abundant mercy blot out my transgressions. Wash me thoroughly from my iniquity and cleanse me from my sin! For I know my transgressions, and my sin is ever before me."

May they be teachable

Proverbs 13:1: "A wise son hears his father's instruction, but a scoffer does not listen to rebuke."

May they be a servant to others

Philippians 2:3–4: "Do nothing from selfish ambition or conceit, but in humility count others more significant than yourselves. Let each of you look not only to his own interests, but also to the interests of others."

May they trust God for their future mate and ministry

Proverbs 3:5–6: "Trust in the LORD with all your heart, and do not lean on your own understanding. In all your ways acknowledge him, and he will make straight your paths."

May they remain pure for their future mate and may their future mate remain pure for them

1 Corinthians 6:18–20: "Flee from sexual immorality. Every other sin a person commits is outside the body, but the sexually immoral person sins against his own body. Or do you not know that your body is a temple of the Holy Spirit within you, whom you have from God? You are not your own, for you were bought with a price. So glorify God in your body."

May they surrender heart and life completely to God

Romans 12:1–2: "I appeal to you therefore, brothers, by the mercies of God, to present your bodies as a living sacrifice, holy and acceptable to God, which is your spiritual worship. Do not be conformed to this world, but be transformed by the renewal of your mind, that by testing you may discern what is the will of God, what is good and acceptable and perfect."

May they be free from bitterness

Hebrews 12:15: "See to it that no one fails to obtain the grace of God; that no 'root of bitterness' springs up and causes trouble, and by it many become defiled."

May they be strong in the Lord

Ephesians 6:10: "Be strong in the Lord and in the strength of his might."

May they be protected from harm

Psalms 17:8–9: "Keep me as the apple of your eye; hide me in the shadow of your wings, from the wicked who do me violence, my deadly enemies who surround me."

May they be protected from accidents

Psalms 91:11–12: "For he will command his angels concerning you to guard you in all your ways. On their hands they will bear you up, lest you strike your foot against a stone."

May they have freedom from fear

2 Timothy 1:7: "God gave us a spirit not of fear but of power and love and self-control."

May they have good health

Psalms 103:2–3: "Bless the Lord, O my soul, and forget not all his benefits, who forgives all your iniquity, who heals all your diseases."

May they always feel loved

Jeremiah 31:3: "I have loved you with an everlasting love; therefore I have continued my faithfulness to you."

May they grow spiritually and walk with God always

Colossians 1:9–10: "And so, from the day we heard, we have not ceased to pray for you, asking that you may be filled with the knowledge of his will in all spiritual wisdom and understanding, so as to walk in a manner worthy of the Lord, fully pleasing to him, bearing fruit in every good work and increasing in the knowledge of God."

May they have a close relationship with each other

Romans 12:10: "Love one another with brotherly affection. Outdo one another in showing honor."

May they develop a hunger for the things of God

Mathew 5:6: "Blessed are those who hunger and thirst for righteousness, for they shall be satisfied."

May they always follow truth and reject lies

3 John 1:4: "I have no greater joy than to hear that my children are walking in the truth."

May they have a love and desire for learning

Proverbs 1:7: "The fear of the LORD is the beginning of knowledge; fools despise wisdom and instruction."

May their speech be God-honoring

Proverbs 13:3: "Whoever guards his mouth preserves his life; he who opens wide his lips comes to ruin."

May they be an example for others to follow

1 Timothy 4:12: "Let no one despise you for your youth, but set the believers an example in speech, in conduct, in love, in faith, in purity."

May they live in the joy of the Lord

Psalm 118:24: "This is the day that the LORD has made; let us rejoice and be glad in it."

May they have no ungodly strongholds

2 Corinthians 10:3–4: "For though we walk in the flesh, we are not waging war according to the flesh. For the weapons of our warfare are not of the flesh but have divine power to destroy strongholds."

Scripture quotations in this section are from the ESV® Bible (The Holy Bible, English Standard Version®), © 2001 by Crossway, a publishing ministry of Good News Publishers. Used by permission. All rights reserved. The ESV text may not be quoted in any publication made available to the public by a Creative Commons license. The ESV may not be translated in whole or in part into any other language.

ACKNOWLEDGMENTS

A wholehearted thank you to:

Our dedicated and supportive husbands—John Goyer and David Nunnery.

Our children . . . we wouldn't have this book without you!

Our consummate agent—Janet Grant. Thank you for believing in us. And the wonderful folks at Moody—Catherine Parks, Pam Pugh, and all the wonderful team members. What a joy to work on this with all of you!

NOTES

1. Hilary Nobilo, "Explaining Social and Emotional Changes During Adolescence," *Brainwave Trust*, https://brainwave.org.nz/article/explaining-social-and-emotional-changes-during-adolescence/.

2. "Mental Health of Adolescents," World Health Organization, October 10, 2024, https://www.who.int/news-room/fact-sheets/detail/adolescent-mental-health.

3. "Suicide: Pediatric Mental Health Minute Series," American Academy of Pediatrics, https://www.aap.org/en/patient-care/mental-health-minute/suicide/.

4. A couple of good resources are *Screens and Teens: Connecting with Our Kids in a Wireless World* by Kathy Koch; and *Screen Kids: 5 Relational Skills Every Child Needs in a Tech-Driven World* by Gary Chapman and Arlene Pellicane.

5. For more information on true gender confusion or dysphoria, consider the book *Trans-Formation: A Former Transgender Responds to LGBTQ* by Dr. Linder Seiler.

6. Tricia Goyer, "How to Stop Your Child's Angry Cycle," *Focus on the Family*, https://www.focusonthefamily.com/parenting/how-to-stop-your-childs-angry-cycle/.

7. For more help and resources to help kids with anger, check out Tricia's book *Calming Angry Kids: Help and Hope for Parents in the Whirlwind*.

8. https://barna.gloo.us/reports/guiding-children-chapter-1. Also see "Who Is Responsible for Children's Faith Formation?," Barna, March 19, 2019, https://www.barna.com/research/children-faith-formation/.

9. Sarah Snuggs and Kate Harvey, "Family Mealtimes: A Systematic Umbrella Review of Characteristics, Correlates, Outcomes and Interventions," *Nutrients* 15, no. 13 (2023): 2841, https://doi.org/10.3390/nu15132841.

10. Kari Ure, "The Power of Family Mealtime," Utah State University, https://extension.usu.edu/relationships/faq/the-power-of-family-mealtime.

11. "Filament Bibles" (from Tyndale House Publishers), which come with a free app, are a good resource for Bible reading with preteens. The app opens up study materials to go with every page of the Bible.

12. Tricia Goyer, "Why do you think active listening is important when it comes to parenting?," Facebook, June 1, 2024, https://www.facebook.com/tricia.goyer/posts/pfbid02xfJLqrDRLauRqFviiTPdy88dxXtSgVkVr9GcwpRgvDWJ3npEtCM-brKNAvU5UZqWrl.

13. https://barna.gloo.us/reports/guiding-children-chapter-1.

14. "Study: Most Evangelicals Chose Christ During Childhood," *Baptist Standard,* February 1, 2024, https://www.baptiststandard.com/news/faith-culture/most-evangelicals-chose-christ-during-childhood-study-shows/.

15. Don Everts and Doug Schaupp, *I Once Was Lost: What Postmodern Skeptics Taught Us About Their Path to Jesus* (IVP Books, 2008).

16. Kathryn A. Kerns et al., "Peer Relationships and Preadolescents' Perceptions of Security in the Child-Mother Relationship," *Developmental Psychology* 32, no. 3 (1996): 457–66, https://doi.org/10.1037/0012-1649.32.3.457.

17. If you would like a download of the Scriptures in this section, go to https://teachthemdiligently.net/resources/prayers-for-my-children/. Reprinted here with permission.

TEACH THEM
Diligently®

Helping Christian parents establish multi-generational impact through biblical, discipleship-driven parenting.

EVENTS, PODCAST, COMMUNITY, BOOKS, AND MORE DESIGNED TO STRENGTHEN YOUR FAMILY AND HELP YOU GIVE YOUR CHILDREN A FAITH THAT STICKS.

Get a Free Faith That Sticks Workshop by Leslie and Tricia at
www.TeachThemDiligently.net/FTS

@teachdiligently

/teachthemdiligently